Understanding God

The Joy of Finally Hearing God's
Good and Gracious Word

❦

Tom Cleary

ISBN 979-8-88540-844-8 (paperback)
ISBN 979-8-88540-845-5 (digital)

Christian Faith Publishing
832 Park Avenue
Meadville, PA 16335
www.christianfaithpublishing.com

All biblical citations from the New Revised Standard Version. Used with permission.

Printed in the United States of America

For Lori, who brought me back through the door,
Pastor Ken, who bolted me to the floor.

May God's peace be with
you always

T-C.

Contents

Preface...vii
1 Foundation and Framework 1
2 Full-Immersion Catholic..11
3 Not Catholic, Jesuit...27
4 Worshipping the Bottle 45
5 Cognitive Dissonance: Failing to Renew...................63
6 Lost in the Wilderness..67
7 Thunder from God's Distant Shore 82
8 Getting Bolted to the Floor 96
9 Turns Out You Have to Keep Listening to God.........104
10 Toward a Re-reformation.......................................126
Notes 171

Preface

This effort is not about proving that God exists. I have been on both sides of that line, and while I have what I consider good philosophical reasons for holding that there is in fact a God, this is neither the time nor the place for such a conversation. Therefore, this effort is for those who are already among the faithful. I would count among that group those who claim to be unsure (agnostic), simply because if they have not outright denied the existence of God, then there is still a level of belief within them. Also included in this group are those who claim that they *want* to believe. I would submit to these folks that they already are faithful; they just have not found its full expression…yet. They have just not fully understood what God is saying to them, but I suspect they desperately want to. This work is especially for them.

This work embodies a life experience that saw me repeatedly stopping listening to God because, in retrospect, I simply did not understand what He was saying to me. I realize that this is not the experience of everyone, but I deeply suspect that more match this experience than do not. If this is your experience, then this work is also for you. If it is not, it hopefully can help explain those in your life who seem to always misunderstand the message that God is seeking them. Additionally, if you are or were Catholic, then this is also for you, as you should find much of my experience growing up Catholic very familiar.

I use a framework that makes sense to me, perhaps it will for you as well. This framework has helped me understand how God called to me and what I can and ultimately did to have a relationship with Him, as well as what I need to keep doing to maintain that relationship.

Obviously, no analogy or framework is perfect, and that includes the one that that I use. However, it is my prayerful hope that a framework that makes so much sense to me and holds such explanatory power for my experience might be of help to those trying to figure out who it is that is chasing them, and what He is trying to get them to understand.

This is not, nor is it intended to be, a work of technical theology. Yes, I am aware of many of the more esoteric concepts of systematic theology in both the Catholic and Protestant traditions, yet I make no pretense to be a trained theologian. This is a work of what I would call "street-level theology." That said, I do focus on one area of technical theology, which is the crux of much misunderstanding. If it is not beyond my grasp, it is not beyond the grasp of anyone. These misunderstandings of what God is telling us occur, with the exception I just mentioned, not at the nuanced level of formal theology, but rather at the level of application (or bastardization). This is the kind of application that occurs at the street level, so to speak. In the final analysis, we live out our lives at this street level and must deal with how these concepts are applied, so that is where this work is centered. The true, necessary fight to spread God's word is indeed a "street thing," so I make no apologies for the orientation of this effort.

As for those who will dismiss this effort because I am not a trained theologian or have not spent X number of years in school or do not have X number of letters after my name, I claim only to be among that class of people known as the priesthood of all believers. That seems good enough for me. If there is any dispute or disagreement, I welcome the conversation. However, I refuse to have a discussion regarding credentials. Rather, I will always engage anyone who thinks I am wrong and wishes to show me where and how I am wrong. This is where *I* stand, and I can do no other.

1

Foundation and Framework

A brief word on what He is saying

I wish to be clear so that there is no misunderstanding. I have a particular view of what God is so clearly saying and what for so long I misunderstood. This misunderstanding is as much my fault as anyone else's, but it did partly result from a garbled message being delivered to me.

It is beyond doubt to me that what I understood as being God's message was gross error. The message I heard, as I shall detail below, is that there were things we should and must do *in order to* gain salvation. This misunderstanding resulted in decades of *cognitive dissonance*, the gap between what I thought I was supposed to do and what I did, the result being unworthiness of God.

The truth I came to understand is, as I quote from Martin Luther, that we cannot *do anything* to make ourselves worthy of God. The good news is *we do not have to*! God freely gives us everything. Jesus came to earth, became human like us, and experienced everything that we as humans experience. That is how much God loves us, wants a relationship with us, and how hard He is trying to communicate with us. All we need is to *believe*. The life, death, and resurrection of Jesus place within us the faith that puts us right with God. This is the truth that I so long misunderstood.

I realize that this is at odds with many theological formulations, particularly those that swirl about the Catholic world, although not exclusive to Catholics. The Catholic Church itself claims that what I have outlined is a misleading oversimplification and a mistake for Protestants to say to Catholics that they believe in faith alone and Catholics believe in "faith and works." To quote Catholic.com, "you will cause him to think that the Catholic Church teaches something that, in fact, it says is false."[1] Yet on that same web page, the church outlines its position by directly quoting from the decree handed down by the Council of Trent, which ran from 1545–1563 and was the church's main theological response to Luther's challenge.

In its *Decree on Justification* produced at the Council of Trent, the church holds that (I am again quoting from the Catholic.com site) "after discussing the justification that occurs at the beginning of the Christian life, Trent quotes several passages from St. Paul on how Christians grow in virtue by yielding our bodies to righteousness for sanctification. It states that by good works we 'increase in that justice received through the grace of Christ and are further justified'" (DJ 10).[2] Let me translate. There are extra works you must *do* to be justified.

Suffice it to say, at some level, the Catholic Church holds that there are works we must perform. I in no way dismiss the sincerity and faithfulness of this group of believers. I simply disagree with them and contend that they have not fully understood what God is saying to us.

Let me also take a moment to make it clear that Catholics are by no means the only ones who take this position. While they are foremost in taking such a formal stand on this issue, all manner of Protestant groups have let these ideas seep into their discourse. An outstanding Lutheran theologian, Gerhard Forde in his powerful book *Where God Meets Man*[3] spoke eloquently to the idea amongst many Protestants of what he termed "ladder theology." This is the idea that we must climb a ladder to God rung by rung. As you may guess from the title of his book, we do not need to as God came here in human form.

The infestation of works righteousness is not limited to Lutherans either. It permeates almost every corner of the Christian world. Most

Christians, if asked what they must do to gain salvation, would answer with some form of works. Lutherans, Anglicans, and any of the various denominations all have millions who would give a works-based answer. I would include the more fundamentalist congregations of the Christian world as well. This would include those of a more fundamentalist mindset who think they need to "decide for Christ," as if there is a question about whether Christ should be believed. Also prominent are those who preach a thing called the "prosperity gospel" or, as it is sometimes called, "name it and claim it" theology. These are the preachers, usually televangelists, who say that if you "believe" enough (as demonstrated by a check to said preacher), then God will give you good things, like a nice house or a car.

All the various manifestations of works righteousness from the more theologically sophisticated Catholic version to the stealthy Lutheran versions to the "deciders for Christ," to the cruder slot machine Jesus fundamentalists, have one thing in common: they seek to manipulate God. They reduce salvation to a transaction. If I do something, then God will give me something. If I push the right button or pull the right lever, then God gives me what I want. It looks like worship, but it puts us firmly in control.

My point in discussing how widespread this idea of works righteousness is, is to steer one away from a simplistic Catholic bashing, as the pernicious idea of works righteousness is like horse manure—all over the place.

Why any of this matters

This matters because works righteousness is a spiritual, theological, and emotional dead end. It produces a cognitive dissonance, which the dictionary defines as "the state of having inconsistent thoughts, beliefs, or attitudes, especially as relating to behavioral decisions and attitude change." This revelation exposes hypocrisy. Hypocrisy is a difficult, nearly impossible thing to live with for very long.

We eventually get to the point that Martin Luther describes as "evangelical despair," which is the giving up of all hope that we can justify ourselves to God with works. When you get to this point, you

3

can go one of two ways, either you solve the problem the way Martin Luther did and clearly understand what God is saying to you, or you can drift/walk/run away from God. It is not simply that I buckled under the weight of works righteousness; it broke me. Only understanding the gospel made me whole again.

This break with God occurs, I think, from one of two causes. Either you cannot live with your own hypocrisy of not being able to meet an impossible standard of works, and/or you cannot live with the fact that those who preach works righteousness fail to live up to this standard.

It is my firm belief that this is the main driver of the decline of self-identified Christians, particularly in the West. In the United States alone, ex-Catholics amount to, by best estimates, around thirty million people, or about 10 percent of the US population. Note, these people are not part of a different faith tradition; they are simply not active in their faith at all. There are multiple memes and even websites and social media groups based on being an ex-Catholic.

There are many specific reasons for people leaving the Catholic Church. People identify church positions on abortion, birth control, same sex marriage, or other such issues. Obviously, the sex abuse scandal plays prominently into this as well. What these positions have in common is that they center around the works that the church performs that in the minds of many members falls egregiously short of a godly standard. Since these folks have been told something that God did not say, namely that you can be justified by works, it should not be surprising that this is the result. I find it sad beyond words that so many would define themselves by what they are not.

This drifting is not limited to Catholics, however. There has been a decided drift away from traditional expressions of Christian faith into either nonbelief or a generalized spirituality, which amounts mostly to not actively engaging with God.

In perusing articles and studies of this phenomenon, the reasons are very similar. In fact, they are not dissimilar from why Catholics leave. It usually centers around the idea the Christians are judgmental hypocrites who do not practice what they preach. It strikes me now as axiomatic that if you preach a message of works righteousness, there is no way you could ever practice it. Who can blame anyone for not wanting to be around hypocrites?

The other main phenomenon that drives people away is the reaction from the prosperity gospel believers. They are preached a message that if they "believe" (by sending a check!), then good things will befall them. When life takes a large dump on them, they begin to think that the whole message as well as the God thing was a lie. God does not lie, but it looks like that when you do not understand what He is saying to you.

The danger, as I outline below, is that the cognitive dissonance that I experienced is so widespread that it drives people away from God because they cannot reconcile the standard of behavior (works) with the reality of our lives. Too many respond as I did by shutting off God's message and drifting off into an arid desert of unbelief.

I claim no special uniqueness to my story. If I thought for a moment that my story was unique, I would not waste anyone's time with telling it. I would simply write it all off to being an outlier or a one-off. However, I cannot help but be of the conviction that my story is decidedly *not* unique. What happened to me has and continues to happen to millions of people. My story is a microcosm of the damaging effects of the theology of works. It is therefore my hope that I can offer those in a similar situation a path out by helping them understand what God is telling us.

The main point here is that we must recognize there is precious good news in realizing that we continually fail to meet God's standard of approval. There is no grace in any of that message, which is why this is not what God is saying to us. The good news comes when we realize that we do not have to do works to get God to love us; we only must accept the freely given gift of His love and grace. This clearer understanding turns the equation on its head. We will try (as best we feebly can) to do good works. However, we do these good works in response to the gift of salvation. That is, we do what we do *because* of God's gift, not *in order* to receive the gift. This clearer understanding of God's message changes absolutely everything. It wipes away the cognitive dissonance and allows us to have the kind of relationship with God that He desires for all His children.

TOM CLEARY

A final thought on the whole Catholic thing

Much of my story centers on the Catholic Church. Sorry, I can't change the fact that I was born, baptized, educated, and raised Catholic. None of what follows should be considered anti-Catholic screed. I am *not* an ex-Catholic. I refuse to define myself by a negation. I *am* a follower of Jesus the Christ in the Lutheran tradition. I only go to great pains to point this out because there are many who would dismiss the point I am making by writing it off as an anti-Catholic psychosis.

I continue to have high regard for those many faithful Catholics who are in my life, which is most of my friends and all my first friends. I deeply respect the ministry that is being performed by many faithful Catholics and respect the helpfulness of many Catholic traditions. I also am impressed by the large body of scholarship befitting a two thousand plus-year-old institution that has thought a lot about a great many important issues.

That said, I do have differences with Catholic dogma. That should not result in a breakdown of a needed conversation, as I think there are many points of ecumenical unity that can be emphasized. Yet there remain differences, and I am not going to ignore the fact that, at a doctrinal level, I think the Catholic Church is not communicating clearly what God is telling us. I point out that I can say that about a great many Protestants as well.

While it is very likely the case that there is less theological difference than meets the eye between Catholics and Protestants, the reality remains that by the time the message gets to street level, it has become simplified into an obey-in-order-to-be-saved ethic, and it then becomes a cudgel to threaten the flock with to maintain order and discipline. That remains a fundamental part of my story, and I can only tell my story.

I know that taking this stand may turn off many people before they have heard the full story of the consequences of misunderstanding God. I would only ask, especially my Catholic brethren, to hear me out. I have walked the walk of a garbled theology and nearly lost my soul in the process. I suspect many of you may have experi-

6

enced something similar. In any event, it cannot harm one to listen to another perspective and see how it may fit one's own experience. However, this is quite enough theology for the moment.

The framework

The framework for this effort is the notion that God is in pursuit of all of us and is trying to communicate with each of us. The idea being that He loves us more than we could possibly love Him and that He wants a relationship with us more than we could possibly want a relationship with Him.

There are, of course, others in the world with us. God is communicating with them as well. Some of these people have already understood what God has been saying to them all along, many from the very beginning. These are the lifelong faithful, Christians from birth. Of these I am admittedly envious.

Then there are those who are being talked to by God, who themselves are trying to communicate with God. These are the seekers. Some are successful and collide joyously with our Lord; others fail to understand God's message (I have been one of these, as we shall see) and stop listening to God and go off in an unfruitful direction.

There are also those in the world who are encouraging us to speak with God and/or allow ourselves to listen to God, as they have done or are doing. Some of them are more effective than others. Some are seemingly behind us, pushing us forward to talk with God (I have been one of these as well). This strikes me as not the best approach. It is like being on an elevator with an earnest believer who is going to take the ride from the lobby to the top floor while grabbing you by the collar and telling you all about this amazing news he must share. These folks are totally well intentioned but lacking a sustainable tactic.

The more effective approach is taken by those who encourage us to listen to God and/or allow ourselves to hear what God is saying to us. They do this by sharing the joy they experience and truly want us to experience that joy for ourselves. This is more likely to produce longer term success than pushing and shoving people along.

Then there is a group of people who are actively closing their hearts, minds, and ears to God, and are encouraging you to do the same (yes, I have been in this group as well). As I painfully discovered, there is nothing at the end of this path but dust. These groups are typically either outright atheists or perhaps those who have had a searing experience with a faith group made up of the last group I wish to discuss.

These folks are communicating with someone other than God. They may *think* they are speaking with God, but they are chasing the other one. They are communicating division, hate, exclusion, and intolerance. They have a deeply fundamentalist (as opposed to a conservative or traditionalist) bent, and fundamentalism is always about who to exclude and who to hate and who to fear. It is best to steer clear of both groups until you have fully understood what God is saying to you.

There are, of course, those who are communicating with God via a variety of confessions. This is true within the Christian community, as witnessed by the variety of denominations. It is also true *outside* of the Christian community, as evidenced by Jews, Muslims, Hindus, and so forth. God *is* pursuing all these people too. As Christians, we fully believe that we are saved by our faith in the risen Lord, Jesus the Christ. However, I would caution that we do not know whom else God may save unto Himself. Nor should we care, as this is *totally* God's business. My only claim is that all other people on the planet are being pursued by God and loved by God as much as He pursues and loves us as Christians. Remember, "for he so loved the world."

The question arises: Why do people shut out the voice of God? The two answers that I think are most common are cognitive dissonance and loss of control. The main reason people shut out God is the cognitive dissonance that I spoke of earlier. When faced with their own behavior that fails the standard or when faced with the behavior of others, especially those in spiritual leadership, that fails the standard, the response is to level a charge of hypocrisy. This charge should not be unexpected nor is it unreasonable, given most people's misunderstanding of a garbled message. Once we clearly understand what God is saying, this objection goes away. That still leaves the issue of control, but that is a much easier thing to deal with.

The resistance to giving up control is a real one. To start listening to and understanding God is to admit that He is in control. This does not sit well with many people. I know it did not sit well with me. We all like to think and are happiest when we feel in control of our lives. We decide what to do, where to go, and which direction our lives take. To give yourself up to God is to recognize that He is in charge. It becomes about following the will of God, not our own whims.

We immediately recognize that we must live for others and sacrifice and serve. We know what it is that God asks because we know what it is that Jesus did. To put others before ourselves, and especially to do as God would have us do, is terrifying. Many would feel like an escaped convict who, exhausted, gives up running from the hounds and guards and submits to captivity. This is not what understanding God is, as I found out, but it seems to be the main motivator of why we close ourselves off from a relationship with God.

Again, in all cases, God is communicating with us. His very presence in the world is His gift and He wants to share that gift with all His children. As Jesus said in Luke 12:32, "It is your Father's good pleasure to give you the kingdom." God is ever-present in our world, seeking a relationship with all of us. All we can do is to start listening and allow God to communicate clearly with us. Those helping us, effectively or not, are also His gift and represent His speaking to us. Those who have understood from the beginning, the lifelong faithful, are also a gift from God.

In the final analysis, it is *all* about God. As Jesus taught in John 15:16, "You did not choose me but I chose you." Martin Luther was even more blunt about this when he wrote in the *Small Catechism*.

> I believe that I cannot by my own reason or strength believe in Jesus Christ, my Lord, or come to Him; but the Holy Spirit has called me by the Gospel, enlightened me with His gifts, sanctified and kept me in the true faith. In the

same way He calls, gathers, enlightens, and sanc-
tifies the whole Christian church on earth, and
keeps it with Jesus Christ in the one true faith.[4]

God speaks to us, God gives us everything as a gift, and God desperately wants access to our lives because He loves us more than we could ever possibly love Him. All those He puts in our lives and all that He places within us represents one long call for us to stop shutting Him out and to give God access to all our lives. All we need to do is to stop closing our minds and allow God to speak clearly to us and uplift us into a full and joyous relationship with Him and with one another. This is an easier thing to say than do, as my own witness will spell out.

2

Full-Immersion Catholic

Rules, rules and then more rules

I was pursued by God from before I was born. God does everything on earth through the people He puts around us. This is true even if the family situation is difficult. There are always people of God interacting with us in His name. This was obviously true in my case, as I came into the world as part of a very religious family setting. I came into the world in 1963 to parents who were living the Catholic dream. I say this because I was the youngest of eight. Having that many in our family was not a particularly notable thing in the Catholic world I stepped into. Most families had at least six. It was not until you got into the area of twelve or thirteen kids in a family that you started to think of a large family unit.

My parents were best described as pre-Vatican Catholics. Pre-Vatican *I*, that is. To say they were traditionalist and conservative Catholics is not to do justice to those terms. They obeyed all the strictures of the Catholic Church: Mass every Sunday and Holy Day of Obligation, knowing *all* the prayers by heart. That includes not just the prayers said every week at Mass but all the prayers associated with the Catholic Rosary and, of course, every funeral prayer there is.

Prayers are, of course, but a part of the Immersive Catholic experience. There is a lengthy list of dos and don'ts that regulate everyday Catholic life. No meat on Fridays during Lent comes immediately

11

to mind. That came about only in 1966, so for the entirety of my parents' upbringing, there was no meat every Friday. Consequently, growing up we had a nonmeat dish on most Fridays regardless of the time of year. To this day, mac and cheese smells like a Friday night to me.

Mass was also a critical part of the Catholic experience, on Sundays and Holy Days of Obligation, of which it seemed there was an endless number. We never really comprehended what those holy days were commemorating, just that we had to go to Mass once again. Mass itself was somewhat dreary, perhaps because it was framed as a thing we *had* to do rather than a thing we *got* to do. I do not doubt that it held great meaning for my parents and many others in attendance; it is simply that this deep meaning was never communicated to us, and Mass was simply another box on the checklist.

Mass itself had a bevy of rules all unto itself. Besides the obvious don't talk in church, there were a series of legalistic rules. The most prominent surrounded communion. You were not supposed to eat within one hour of receiving communion. I have never been presented with the why of this requirement. In fact, I am not sure it was officially part of Catholic teaching, yet every adult assumed that this was the rule, so for all intents and purposes, it was. It was really the spiritual equivalent of not going swimming until at least thirty minutes after eating, or you would cramp up and die.

What these rules produced was a series of ridiculous questions directed at clergy and teachers. Questions such as "Is it an hour before communion (about three fourths of the way through Mass) or, is it an hour from the start of Mass?" Answer: Probably an hour before communion itself, but just to be safe, make it an hour before Mass. Or the weighty questions about fluids. Is water okay? Yes. Is juice okay? No. How about medicines? Yes. What about toothpaste (this was actually asked of my fifth-grade teacher)? The answer? Yes, but only if you did not swallow (Hand to God, this is true. I cannot make this up). Legalism is a crucial part of a fully immersed Catholic experience.

The other set of rules that was highlighted in the Catholic tradition concerned sex. These were not rules that were spelled out in detail. There was no sex education per se in my time in Catholic grade school. There was just an underlying assumption that sex was only for married people and more or less a necessary evil at that. The vacuum of sex knowledge was filled in with the usual hoary tales of blindness and hairy palms due to masturbation, not to mention the opprobrium of genteel society if these nefarious activities were discovered.

Also filling in the knowledge gap were the usual suspects: *Playboy* magazine and its coarser cousins. Getting ahold of these was easier than one might think because of the dynamic of prohibition. If it was proscribed, morally certainly but also legally to a large degree, then getting to these was as easy as finding an older sibling's stash or a convenience store with a cashier who was lenient.

So the rule about sex as dirty led to a sex education fueled by porn (it hardly seems that compared to today's variety) and my sister's copy of *Our Bodies, Ourselves*.

The other aspect of the Catholic rules regarding sex was the attitude toward gays. To be fair, this was a generalized societal attitude that extended beyond the Catholic Church. The assumption was, of course, that any type of same-sex behavior was wrong and dirty. The usual schoolyard epithets were delivered to anyone who seemed effeminate or odd. In time, it became just a generalized put-down delivered without any greater meaning than that. Yet, in the process, it eliminated any who felt differently about their sexuality from full participation in the community. The *rule* was more important than any one individual; that much we knew in our bones.

Hell was, of course, the underlying enforcer to all these rules. Apparently, Catholics believed the stick to be a better motivator than the carrot. Like many of the rules, hell was not spoken of much in a direct manner. It was just assumed.

There was more talk of purgatory than hell. For the uninitiated, purgatory was between heaven and hell and was where you went if you were not condemned but not quite ready to enter the "show." In purgatory you got purified. I remember seeing images of people being very slowly released from purgatory a bit at a time, their bodies straining up toward heaven until, at last, the foot was released, and they sailed up to the pearly gates. The underlying assumption was that most were going to purgatory, except for the especially virtuous.

For me, the idea of limbo was worse than either hell or purgatory. Limbo was the doctrine (I say was because Catholics don't hold this anymore) that if an infant died before he or she was baptized, he or she would go to limbo. It never made much sense to me. I mean, if you were innocent, why would God want no relationship with you. However, the truly terrifying thing was that it sounded terminally boring. I always pictured the inhabitants of limbo simply hanging in one place with absolutely nothing going on for all eternity. This was a doctrine aimed at young parents to get them to baptize their children in the faith as soon as possible.

Rules and their hellish enforcement, officially and unofficially, were one pillar of a fully immersive Catholic upbringing. The other was the nearly total insularity of this existence.

Insulated, you know…like the mob

To grow up in a fully immersed Catholic world was to be surrounded in almost every phase of your life by the church and its institutions. It reminds me of one of the scenes in *Goodfellas* where Karen Hill was talking about her social world: "There were never any outsiders around. Absolutely never." That was the Catholic world I grew up in.

It was not just about going to Mass on Sundays and Holy Days of Obligation. School was Catholic, and all extracurricular activities were associated with school. Any sports you played were played on the parish team. All your friends were from school and the parish. It can be fairly said that the totality of your social existence ran through and amongst the church and her various branches.

All of this was simply normal; it did not feel odd, because it was all we ever knew. This exposes what I think is a misconception amongst non-Catholics. There is an assumption that Catholics bashed other faith traditions in their clear desire to claim exclusivity for the Catholic confession. This is erroneous. I cannot remember a time when either a cleric or lay teacher ever disparaged another faith tradition. They simply *never* talked about them at all...*ever*. Protestants and Jews (Muslims not a blip on the radar at this point) might as well have not existed. We never associated with non-Catholics, and we never heard them talked about. From our insular world, they did not in fact exist.

This is critical to understanding the Catholic experience. All aspects of your life were dominated by the church. Your education, your social life, your sports life, everything revolved around your faith life. That was, of course, just the way the church wanted it. Rules-based insularity was what they considered to be the most effective tool of maintaining the flock intact.

I will speak in a moment of what has become of this model, but one should not underestimate its impact. The world we lived in created a legion of "cultural Catholics." This cultural Catholicism has and I think will long outlast the rules and even the dogma of the church. A quick example will show what I mean. I ran into the brother of a classmate of mine from a large Catholic family. It is the nature of Catholic relationships that you know not only the one who is your age but also their parents, siblings, cousins, and the like. You are friends with entire families, not just a single individual. In catching up with this man, I learned that his two children were at a Catholic grade school. This was surprising as this person had long been an openly avowed atheist. He then proceeded to tell me that this grade school was up in his grill about the fact that his children were not baptized. So not only was he still a nonbeliever, so was his wife; otherwise, the children would have been baptized. Yet he sent his children to Catholic school. This was not in a town like Chicago where the public school system was so awful that parochial school was a better option no matter what your beliefs. Such is the power of cultural Catholicism that even atheists are held in its thrall.

I need to digress briefly. These rules and the insularity that accompanied them are driven by the Catholic doctrine of faith and works. This is more derogatively referred to as works righteousness. Yes, Catholics will tell you that you need faith to be saved by God through Christ, and I believe them. Yet, at some level, you must perform works as well to attain salvation. This is in contrast with

Protestant theology, which holds that we do good works *because* we have been given salvation, not *in order* to attain salvation. This distinction, unknown to me as a youth, would loom large later.

A nineteenth-century model

I only bring it up to point out that Catholic dogma and theology were completely consistent with the rules-based insularity that they built. The two totally reinforced each other. This was a dogma that existed from almost the beginning but was sharpened during the Counter-Reformation. The model that I have detailed was long in the making, and in the US, it required a certain critical mass of Catholics in the population to work. This did not occur until the latter part of the nineteenth century, during the period of high immigration from heavily Catholic countries such as Ireland, Italy, and Poland.

When the Catholic population grew large enough to sustain parochial schools and a multitude of parishes and ministry activities, the model was complete. I would mark its completion in 1885, with the publication of the *Baltimore Catechism*, and was based on Robert Bellarmine's 1614 *Small Catechism*. This was *the* standard text from 1885 until the late 1960s. My parents' generation knew it by heart, and it provided the dogmatic foundation of the Catholic world I inhabited. Its rise and fall mirrored the rise and ultimate fall of the rules-based insularity I have outlined.

A brief aside. If you grew up in a small town, then you did not experience full-immersion Catholicism. Yes, you were subject to all the rules, and you were under the thrall of works righteousness, but it was a different lived experience. You would have encountered other faith traditions and would have had to deal with that fact. You would need a population center of about two hundred thousand or greater to experience the full-immersion effect. That said, the experience of most Catholics in this country is such a full-immersion experience because Catholicism in the United States was primarily an urban movement.

This model worked in the United States for most of the twentieth century because for most of that time, this nation was itself insulated from much of the rest of the world. The First World War did not make that much of an impact because relatively few Americans went overseas, and its duration for the US was only about eighteen months. In the aftermath of the war, Europe was ruined, and the United States turned its back on much of the rest of the world.

In 1921 the US significantly tightened its immigration laws and greatly restricted the entry of foreigners into the US. These laws were tightened again in 1924 and would not be loosened significantly until the 1960s. Even involvement with the world via trade was curtailed, as relatively high tariff rates insulated much of the US economy from interaction with the rest of the world. These tariffs would be ratcheted up again in the early 1930s in response to the depression. This was a period when America increasingly turned inward economically, socially, and culturally. This paralleled and fueled the rules-based insularity that was the essence of a fully immersive Catholic experience.

This model began to break down in the aftermath of the Second World War. It is fashionable, especially amongst conservatives to blame much of America's social and cultural problems on the sixties, but the deep changes that created so much angst were born during the war years. The brute fact is that the war changed *everything*.

The model and everything else crack

WWII was a four-year grind for the United States and involved every corner of the country, and its effects touched nearly every citizen. The song "How Ya Gonna Keep 'Em Down on the Farm (After They've Seen Paree?)" was published in 1919 and was an outgrowth of WWI. Its insight came to full fruition after the end of WWII. Millions of service members, men and women, served overseas and were exposed to many different cultures and peoples. They were exposed to horrors that they could not have imagined. To say that it changed them would be an understatement. It would have been shocking if this mass national experience had not deeply altered American culture.

This change occurred even before the sixties. Immediately after the war, the film *The Best Years of their Lives* was released and dealt with the difficult transition that returning service members had. Even such quintessentially fifties movies like *The Man in the Grey Flannel Suit* dealt with the psychological effects of the war years. The fifties saw the rise of *Playboy* magazine and the Beatnik movement, as well as the nascent civil rights movement. This era saw a churning beneath the surface that presaged a profound change in American culture.

True enough, the change would manifest itself not so much in the WWII generation but in their children. Yet it is important to remember that it was the WWII generation that fueled this change as an outgrowth of their war experience. One major component of this fuel was the postwar prosperity that swept across America. The twenty years of the depression and the war had built up a pent-up demand for normal living, and many saw this as just recompense for the US "saving" the world. It was time to live the good life, and live it this nation did. A heretofore level of wealth and comfort was enjoyed by a much wider segment of society than ever before.

The society that was created can for many, at least many more than before, be termed "the no-problem society." Roof over your head: no problem. Food on the table: no problem. Educational opportunities: no problem. Career prospects: no problem. An ever upward set of assumptions settled into the psyche of the American public and led to a generation that assumed all good things and never contemplated failure.

This was the world I was born into in 1963, at the tail end of the baby boom, born to parents who formed a large family in the aftermath of the war and progressed socially along with the times. Yes, they were conservative, yet they clearly evolved with the culture as most do. They certainly had their share of postwar prosperity as my father formed what would be a very successful business forms company in 1958. In short, we wanted for nothing and assumed, like so many others, that the sky was the limit. This was also true of most of the classmates I had who were also living a fully immersed Catholic life.

In such a no-problem world, with all good things assumed and an ever-changing set of mores all around, it would have been odd if the rules-based insular model *didn't* crack. Social change is often easier when you live a cosseted existence. One change that beset the Catholic world was brought on by themselves: Vatican II. While I think this changed the church less than either its supporters or detractors claimed, it did effect significant cultural changes to the church.

The Mass was no longer in Latin but could be understood by the laity. Nuns were no longer absolutely required to wear habits (though most in my world did), and a general lessening of formality spread all around. This was certainly a changed environment for us as Catholic youths even if we never really knew the more stringent version of the model. It must have been emotionally excruciating for the clergy and nuns who were firmly ensconced in the old ways and the old way of discipline.

By the time I entered my grade school years, the seventies was in full bloom.

Vietnam and Watergate revealed that the old truths the nation lived by were gone in a blizzard of lies and corruption. Much of what the country thought they knew suddenly was not so. A deep cynicism descended over the country. We as grade-schoolers were not immune to this. It was rather hard to miss this national implosion in a TV world with only 3 ½ channels (PBS was the half).

Even though we were only ten or eleven years old, we were aware of the outside world. I distinctly remember the day in October 1973 when the principal, Sister Helen David, came on the loudspeaker and announced that Vice President Spiro Agnew had resigned. She then dismissed school for the rest of the day and told us to go home and pray for the nation. It seemed a silly response to me as a ten-year-old (not that today I consider prayer meaningless). It just seemed so *desperate*. In retrospect, it was rather sad—a good decent woman watching all that she knew for the entirety of her life simply melt away. At that moment, however, I was just glad we got a half day off school.

The next year, we saw Watergate consume the rest of the debilitated Nixon presidency (the hearings blew up my 1974 summer TV routine). Then a year later, I remember the fall of Saigon and the awful scenes from the embassy and the helicopters getting tossed off the side of US naval vessels. Thus ended the post-WWII truths upon which our world had been ordered. Gone with it was a generation (even at age ten) that believed this garbage anymore. All truths, even the vaunted rules-based insularity of the Catholic Church, were now in play. The near-century-old model began to look as faded as the old "Fall Out Shelter" sign that still hung on the back stairway of Saint Margaret Mary School.

The problem was my world was still run by a group of lay and religious workers steeped in the old ways and stubbornly clinging to them at what seemed like all cost. Old-school, hardscrabble priests and nuns committed to the established *truths*, confronted by a horde of overprivileged punks who never assumed a downside to life and who were witnessing the dissolving of America's self-identity, would make for a combustible mix.

To understand what this confrontation looks like, it is necessary to spend a bit of time describing the front line of the Catholic experience: nuns. Growing up Catholic, I can tell you that no one loomed larger than the nuns. They were the day-to-day interface with all things Catholic, and they truly seared themselves onto the memory of Catholic youth everywhere. They are one of the chief reasons that the culture of Roman Catholicism runs so deep.

In the Catholic world, it was the nuns who ruled day to day. They could strike fear with a look or a sharp word. One of the reasons I am not particularly afraid of terrorists is that I was educated by nuns. If any nun had been sent to the Middle East armed only with a ruler, I suspect she could have cleared out ISIS within a week. I could fill many pages with stories of what they did to enforce order and orthodoxy. I was witness to many depredations of people's dignity and heard tell of many others from my siblings. Things such as pushing an eraser on the floor with your nose or individuals hung up on a coat hook rack by the back of their shirts or the cries of the victims of a paddling via the "Board of Education."

A few select anecdotes should suffice. Abuse was both physical and mental. One stellar memory is of being in the bathroom in first grade and not paying attention and cranking out a wasteful amount of paper towels from the old-fashioned dispenser. Whereupon my first-grade teacher nun smacked me in the back of the head and dragged me by the ear out of the bathroom. All the while, I could only wonder what in the hell she was doing in the boy's bathroom, as if any area was off-limits to this woman! Another notable memory came from the "librarian" nun. I was tasked with counting the number of zip codes in our metro area in the phone book (don't ask why this is even remotely educational) and inadvertently covered up one with my arm at the bottom of the page. This warranted a smack to the head whereby I discovered my error. It was here that I learned that pain is not an effective pedagogical tool.

One more anecdote should bring into full relief the fear that these women generated. Every class has a skirt lifter; ours was no exception. This young man was told by one of the nuns that if he did this again, he would be slapped across the face. He, of course, transgressed again. Sister did not get angry and impulsively hit him; this I could understand. No, she proceeded to enact a ritual that is as close to an execution that I ever wish to see. In the middle of a playground field, she faced the accused. The field was torn up due to renovations. The girls of the class were at one end, behind some dirt mounds, the boys at the other end, also behind some dirt mounds. Just the two were in the center of the field. This nun started her assault from about her hip, and by the time her hand reached this boy's face, it had serious velocity. She cracked him openhandedly across his face, and he went down like a victim of Muhammad Ali. It was one of the most stunning things I have ever witnessed. The deepness of these events on my memory should be evident by the fact that they occurred more than forty-five years ago. Such is the imprint of a Catholic upbringing.

I was exposed to racism as well. In one instance, my first-grade teacher, a nun, called me up to the front of the class in response to my talking when I was to remain quiet. She proceeded to ream me out in front of the class (because she believed in management by humiliation). She knew my parents employed a black housekeeper because the convent was across the street from our home. She then asked where it was that I picked up my bad habits, "from that Negro cleaning woman I suppose." Or when Sister caught me using the nearby creek as a lavatory and implored me to act better because I was not "some poor Negro child who had to pee behind a tree." At the ages of six and eight years, you only know that there is something wrong with these statements. Some years later, it hits you that these women were racist dirt balls!

And yet...and yet I cannot completely look back on these experiences without some sadness for the plight of these women. The Catholic Church then and now treats them as second-class citizens. These women turned their lives over to Christ in honest faith. That faith was repaid by being shunted into health care or education regardless of training or temperament. So nuns were regularly misemployed and underemployed as well as not being allowed to fully participate in the proclamation of the gospel or the administration of the sacraments. Add to this the fact that they were cut off from any intimate relationships (as are priests) and forced to dress head to toe in black every day. Oh, and let's not forget that there is no retirement plan offered them, so when they are all used up and can work no more, they face their declining years with the real prospect of abject poverty. You live that life for thirty years and see if you don't crack. Smacking some smart-ass punk upside his head becomes a venting tool as much as anything else. This does not excuse the awful things these people did, but it certainly makes it understandable. From understanding should come some sympathy. Given all of this, it is understandable that these people would have difficulty coping with a significantly changed social and cultural milieu.

My career as a smart aleck

I certainly was well suited to fill the part of smart-aleck provocateur. My confrontational period began fully in fifth grade. I am not going to go into detail about how this rebellion manifested itself; that would be a book all its own. It is more important to understand the broad outline of my pushback, a pushback that was not at all just mine.

The main manifestation of my pushback was simply that I was a smart aleck. I was not doing drugs or drinking...yet. I was not violent nor was a truant. In fact, I liked to go to school with the express desire to see what trouble I could stir up. I distinctly remember looking in the mirror some days and wondering what trouble I could cause. I incessantly talked back to my teachers in any manner I felt like at any given moment.

Two anecdotes should suffice to illustrate. In fifth grade, I had a teacher who, as it turned out after his death, appeared on a registry of those with serious allegations of sexual abuse of students on an Indian reservation. That was not my experience with him in grade school. However, if there was a National Registry of the Ineffectual, his name would have been at the top of the list. One day, he announced that if he noticed you using the restroom between classes, he would not allow you to use it again during his class. I immediately raised my hand and asked, "What if someone really has to go?" He responded, "I didn't know you had that sort of problem, Mr. Cleary."

The class right away began to mock me. Making sizzle sounds, as in you got burned Cleary. Right away, you should see what sort of towering intellect we are dealing with here. I mean what a challenge to take on a fifth grader with a juvenile insult. However, it was a challenge, and the gauntlet had been thrown down, and I could not let this challenge go unanswered. I immediately responded that "Every time I look at you, I get sick, so I have to use the restroom." The sizzle sounds were straightaway directed back at our teacher. He stammered a moment then threw me out of the class. Throwing a student out of the class was the grade school version of "going nuclear" and represented a clear win for the student. If all you can offer by way of response is to toss a kid out of class, then you lose.

The next year, I was in detention, which was overseen by the vice principal. This joker was the one who really ran the school as the nun who was the principal was a mere figurehead. The vice principal thought he was a badass because he taught for a couple years at an inner-city high school. Ooh, we were so scared! Now, that I was in detention was not notable, as the vice principal pointed out to me that year that I had sixty-five detentions during the school year. Surprisingly, he was not amused when I joyfully asked him if sixty-five detentions were a record. I maintain to this day that it was in fact a record.

Well Mr. Badass was strutting around detention one day, talking about his inner-city experience and how tough he was, all the while manipulating a rolled-up bunch of papers the way Colonel Klink would wave his riding crop around. He then stated, "I brush my teeth with acid," to which I immediately responded, "That's why you don't have any teeth left." This, of course, got the laughs at his expense that I was seeking. His response was to slap my face with the rolled-up papers he had in his hand. This too represents a clear win. If all you have to offer is violence, you Mr. Badass, lose. I, of course, wasted no time in claiming a massive injury and how my eye must have been put out. Mr. Badass then got nervous and let me go home from detention early. You take whatever wins you can against ineffectual "leaders."

The point of these stories is to reflect on why it is that an elementary school student would even consider talking to an adult like this. Not just any adults but those adults who were specifically in an authority relationship with said student. As I mentioned earlier, I was not alone in this. At one point, fully half of the boys in my seventh-grade section were on probation. They, like me, were not violent nor substance abusers or truants, just a group who felt comfortable in letting whatever smart-aleck comment that was rattling around their heads spew out their piehole.

The two reasons I can come up with to best explain this behavior are the breakdown in the church model due to societal changes and the utter security we had in our world. This security was enhanced in my situation by the unconditional love expressed to me by my parents. I have never met greater practitioners of unconditional love than these two people. I know their love was unconditional because as will be seen a bit later, I put many conditions upon that love, and yet they never abandoned me.

All this rebellion seems remarkably tame by today's standards. I mean, kids in schools today will flat out tell teachers to go screw themselves. However, I suspect that this occurred in some schools even back then. True enough, though, it *was* tame by standards today. I am not claiming it was a mass uprising à la the French Revolution. I am saying that this pushback represented the cracking of the immersive Catholic world that was erected by the end of the nineteenth century. First comes a pushback, then a more generalized questioning of the way things have been done, then a drifting into noncompliance with what the immersive Catholic model demands, then an active walking away from the church altogether. This is exactly what has happened to millions of people who now define themselves by what they are not. The latter part of the twentieth century saw the rise of the ex-Catholic.

As for my experience at pushing back and ignoring the old model, it ended, not surprisingly, with expulsion from Catholic grade school in the last quarter of my seventh-grade year. Even ineffectual teachers and administrators will only tolerate so much. After nearly three years of popping off, being sent to detention, and being put on probation, they finally gave me the boot. Then, as now, I did not question the justice of this, only that if they kicked me out, they should have booted about a dozen other people as well. It was, though, an inexpensive lesson learned early in life: There is only so much garbage you can throw into the face of others before they will put their footprint on your backside. This was a lesson that would serve me well in the years ahead.

Of these years I can conclude that, for the most part, the people talking to me in the name of God were good, decent people. They worked for substandard wages and, in the case of nuns, were treated as second-class citizens of the church. It would be uncharitable to suggest that unlike most people in the world, they did not do the best they could. However, it would be fantasy to say that they were effective pursuers of souls. To shut my ears to them was easy, and it was an environment that made me want to stop listening.

There really are non-Catholics in the world

My next stop after Catholic grade school was public junior high. My dad was correct. Why should he pay extra just to have me screw up? It was here, for the first time in my life, that I came across a sizable number of non-Catholics. These were not nonbelievers as I might have expected. They were people from families that were religiously observant. They were comprised of Episcopalians, Methodists, Congregationalists, and even a Unitarian. One public school classmate went on to become the Episcopalian bishop in this area. I remember having conversations with them about their faith practices, and they with me as a Catholic. My reaction was one of head-scratching bewilderment. I mean, *who* were these people? Religiously, they might as well have been from Mars.

The long-term lesson I learned is that they were regular, good, decent people. They were no different from me or anyone else whom I knew. It would not be a long exposure to a religiously diverse crowd, as my stay in public schools was only a year and a quarter. Getting kicked out of grade school was one thing, but there was no question that I would be headed to the all-boys Catholic high school, the alma mater of my grandfather, father, and all my brothers. Right back into a fully immersed Catholic world—a world run not by Catholics, but rather Jesuits.

3

Not Catholic, Jesuit

What's a Jesuit anyway?

One cannot fully understand the meaning of the title of this chapter if one has not had some lengthy exposure to Jesuits. Yes, of course, they are a Catholic religious order. Yet they are so different as to nearly constitute a separate denomination all unto themselves. To be pursued with a message in the name of God by those wearing the black robes is to be pursued and spoken to by those that mean business.

The Jesuits, or more properly the Society of Jesus, is a Catholic order founded by Ignatius Loyola, Saint Ignatius Loyola that is, in 1534. Loyola's vision and work grew as a direct response to the Protestant Reformation. They were to be the leading edge in the church's response to this challenge. Loyola himself had a military background and had in fact been wounded in battle. It is not surprising then that he used a military style of organization.

Also, military in nature was the rigorous training and discipline required. First, there was a lot of discipline necessary to even become a Jesuit. Today it takes about fourteen years from your first enrollment until your final vows. They have had, from the very beginning, a serious emphasis on education and intellectual rigor, hence the long ordination process. There is also an expectation that your formal education will continue long after ordination. Many Jesuits end up with multiple advanced degrees in a variety of fields.

While the Jesuits were initially about countering the Reformation through evangelization and pastoral ministry, today they are primarily concerned with teaching. Therefore, if you enter the Jesuits, you know that you will most likely be posted to a teaching position. This creates a self-selecting dynamic that is missing when you look at Catholic nuns. This produces a legion of priests and brothers who want to teach and more likely have a facility for teaching. This alone makes them more formidable communicators than nuns and underpaid Catholic lay teachers.

The Jesuits are also more formidable because of the more militant culture that has, from the beginning, marked the Jesuit order. They were conceived as the pope's army or later as papal shock troops. An aggressive stance is part and parcel of what it is to be a Jesuit. This certainly manifested itself in many awful episodes throughout history; their part in the Inquisition and their evangelical activities in the Spanish colonies come immediately to mind.

Theologically, the Jesuits I knew were conservative and orthodox. Politically, they tended to be left of center but not too far left. This is no longer the case today, as many Jesuits have been radicalized into a Marxist economic/political philosophy and a Marxist influenced liberation theology of underclass revolution. Suffice it to say that in my time with the Jesuits, they were traditionalist Catholics who expected you to follow the rules and to be insulated from the rest of the world. This was no different from the full-immersion world I had experienced in grade school, except that these were better educated and more aggressive proponents of the Catholic worldview.

I cannot fault them for their beliefs and do not question their sincerity, for the most part. There were many fine educators and gracious clerics answering a call as their consciences informed them. Overall, I think they were quite a bit more effective than the grade school world I left behind. This attitude is reflected in their motto (possibly informal), "Give us your boys, and they will be our men for life." Many I know have certainly followed this path and are lifelong supporters of the Jesuit way and actively Catholic in their faith walk. This number, however, does not include me. As effective as the Jesuits were, I was ultimately motivated to stop listening to them, although it took more effort than in grade school.

A slow-rolling rebellion

To be clear, at first, I did not try to shut out any of these folks. Prior to entering high school, I was all with the program. I distinctly remember training over the summer (I had taken up track and cross-country) and running past the school and pledging myself to Prep (Omaha Creighton Prep). I look back at those moments with horrified embarrassment. The thought of offering myself to an earthly institution that I really knew little about makes me cringe now. However, at the time, it was what I desired. Perhaps it was my pledge to do better considering my expulsion from grade school, that event being not yet the badge of honor it later became. Perhaps it was an early instance of me seeking to speak with God and seeking something greater than myself. In any event, I was prepared to dive into the deep end of the immersive Catholic experience.

This would not last. It lasted the better part of my freshman year, but the desire to close my ears overtook me. It was like being in the middle of a fog and then seeing clearly as the fog slowly lifted. It occurred to me one day that Prep sucked. I was not at the time sure where this desire to stop listening came from. It is likely that I realized that the Jesuits were, in substance, the same rules-bound automatons I had experienced in grade school. While they were certainly more intellectually rigorous and challenging than any I had come across, yet in the end, they offered a "take it or leave it" worldview.

To share some examples is to reveal the ultimate shallowness of the theology offered up. One day, one of my teachers, who was also the cross-country coach, was pontificating (he always pontificated) about what it took to get into heaven. He analogized this process to earning a letter sweater (yeah, I know!). One got a letter sweater only after fulfilling all the requirements of a varsity athlete. Getting into heaven was the same, he claimed. I mean, he thought it axiomatic that one would not want anyone to receive a varsity letter without earning it, and by extension, nobody would want to inhabit heaven with the unworthy. I knew the moment he offered up this analogy that it was complete and utter nonsense. It seemed and in fact was shallow and feckless. Maybe this was an inchoate leaning toward a Protestant theology of grace, or perhaps it was just a clear recognition of the insipid argument put forth.

Another event from my freshman year immediately put me off and, in the years since, turned my stomach. One of the priests, later to be credibly accused of abuse, came to freshman biology class to discuss the connection between the science and the theology. He had earlier come to discuss the compatibility of God and evolution, a view that made sense then and now. Then one day, he came to class during our study of human reproduction. He arrived to discuss the Catholic position regarding abortion. This struck me as not unreasonable at a Catholic institution. He was dealing with the issue of offering an exception to the prohibition of abortion in cases of rape or incest. I honestly cannot remember what he said about incest because of what he said about rape. First, he talked about how rare it was for women to conceive during a rape, the odds of being fertile at any one time being rather long to begin with. Then he went on to say that the stress and trauma of a rape would likely preclude being able to produce fertile eggs in any event. Therefore, this giant of logic concluded that if some women get pregnant because of rape, it must be because they wanted it. Or as he said, "Some women rape easier than others." In looking back, I now fully realize how disgusting this argument was, but even at the time, I knew it to be garbage and the man who made the argument a manure salesman.

It is interesting to note that this same priest was informally accused of breaking the vow of privacy surrounding the Catholic sacrament of confession. A friend was certain that what he had told this priest about some drinking and pot smoking was told to the administration. He was certain because he got in trouble for it with no other credible source of where the information would have come from. In any event, I never trusted this priest again. History bore me out in this.

These are standout moments, but they were repeated in hundreds of smaller and less offensive ways. Overall, my shutting off God is on me and expresses my weakness as a fallen creature. In the case of my ceasing to listening to these people, I would say it was the right thing to do. These were people you *should* stop listening to. While many were well intentioned, those who offered up the ugliness of what I just shared were the ones that got remembered. These are moments you don't get over easily. In retrospect, what I can say positively is that I was not shutting off God as much as shutting off those who were not preaching any good news at all. That is, I was rejecting a garbled message. That is the problem with ineffectual communicators on God's behalf. If you screw it up, you might push people all the way out from the shadow of the cross. They misunderstand what God is really saying and act on that misunderstanding.

My resistance to what they offered was not nearly so direct as it was in grade school. First, these people were to be taken a lot more seriously than the nuns and lay staff in grade school. Second, I had learned from my grade school expulsion that you could only push people so far before they showed you the door, and I was certain that if I got bounced from high school, a military academy awaited.

Embracing my passive-aggressive self

So I got good at more subtle forms of resistance. I understand it much more clearly now, but what I unknowingly got very good at was passive-aggressive pushback. Outwardly I would nod yes, but inwardly I was shaking my head no. That is not to say that I never pushed back openly, but it tended to be more intellectual resistance than the simple aberrant behavior that marked the grade school me.

The first two years of a regimented existence like Omaha Creighton Prep did not leave a lot of room for intellectual freelancing. The courses were basic and lecture-driven and did not have room for discussion. This is not a knock on the curriculum; it's the same most everywhere and would be true even in the foundational college courses I took. So I spent my time taking all that was delivered to me and filtering it through my brain. By my junior year, I was ready to respond.

Given the more rigorous, serious nature of my high school environment, I took my responses more seriously. I engaged intellectually with those in my world, including teachers and Jesuits. Normally, this took the form of asking questions, at times impertinent ones. In one memorable exchange, a rather insane Jesuit teaching theology (really it was just his view of the world) was going on about how not to get in trouble with girls. Since, he said, people tend to cross whatever boundary they set for themselves, one should draw a tight boundary. In this case, he said do not draw a line at a girl's waist because you will cross it and get into trouble. Rather, he argued, draw the line at her neck so that if you cross it, you will not get into as much trouble. Obviously, he had not thought through the idea that once you cross a boundary, especially a self-imposed one, you will advance as far as you can. The whole attitude was, on reflection, chauvinistic as if the woman involved had no say in the matter. However, my immediate response was to ask him why not just draw the line at a girl's feet so you will never cross it. This question, to say the least, was not appreciated. Upon reflection, it was a reflexive rejection of an inane legalism.

I was not always such a smart aleck. I remember an exchange with a lay teacher who was defending Catholic teaching on contraception, specifically the rhythm method. He was arguing that it was just as effective as other forms of artificial birth control. I had my doubts about that but accepted this as a premise. Then I asked, if it was just as effective as artificial birth control, then what was the moral difference as both methods allow for sex without pregnancy? I recall his response was that the rhythm method was reversible. I countered that any form of birth control except sterilization was reversible; simply stop taking the pill, take off the condom, or lose your sense of rhythm. He was gracious, but we agreed to disagree (that is a *huge* concession in this environment). In any event, it was becoming clearer that I was growing impatient with hairsplitting legalisms that lacked any moral distinctions.

I also challenged hypocrisy when I came across it, not my own, of course, only those of others at this point. One afternoon, before cross-country practice early in the season, the team received the

"Anti-drinking Talk." This was in direct response to a blowout party the previous weekend that saw many athletes (including one dead drunk cross-country team member) observed staggeringly drunk by teachers who got wind of the party and drove by to investigate. Amazingly enough, I was not in attendance but heard all the sordid details. This put the teachers/ coaches into crisis mode, and every team's coach committed to delivering the *talk*. So the Jesuit who was the cross-country coach intoned most seriously about how it was so important to refrain from drinking during the season. Notable was that he emphasized refraining from drinking during the season; the rest of the year was apparently okay.

After his mini-sermon, he went down the line one team member at a time to ask us what we thought. Each one in turn stated unequivocally that it was wrong to drink during the season. What burned me was that even guys I knew who drank during the season went along with the program and told this man what he wanted to hear. This included the guy who was so uproariously drunk just a few days before.

I, as it turned out, was the last one to speak. I thought for a moment and concluded that yes, getting royally drunk during the season was probably not a good idea but that having a beer now and then wasn't going to kill you. Psycho-Jesuit exploded. "Cleary," he yelled, "go over by that tree and be by yourself and think about this." As I went, I quietly suggested that if he wanted me to tell him just what he wanted to hear, he should have let me know. Silly student that I was, I thought he wanted my opinion. I never made that mistake again. It was just a further loosening of the tendrils holding me to the Catholic worldview.

Mostly this time saw me drift into a spiritual apathy. I was old enough to be sent to Mass on Sundays by myself, or so my parents thought. This was a time when I substituted skipping Mass to read political and philosophical tracts. On nice days, I would walk out the driveway, the property being large enough to then put me out of sight. I would then circle to the garage, which sat on the other side of the property. Behind the garage was a shed and behind the shed was enough room to sit and read. It was here that I cut my teeth on classical liberal and libertarian thought and free market economics. This seemed at the time a better use of an hour on Sunday than Mass.

As I got older and was able to drive, I would leave for "Mass" and then drive to church to pick up a bulletin (to prove my attendance) from inside the door. That is, until they got smart and stopped putting the bulletin out until halfway through Mass. After that, I just conveniently "forgot" to pick one up. Then I would drive the interstate loop around the city of Omaha at speeds quite a bit over the limit. Fortunately, the law was not out in force on Sunday mornings nor was much other traffic.

I would occasionally get busted skipping Mass, but mostly my parents did not want to know, so they did not ask too many questions. If I did get caught, I did get the "shame" speech. This happened most memorably on Christmas morning one year. I was ostensibly going to midnight Mass on Christmas Eve, at the all-girls high school my sisters attended. I concocted some excuse why I had to drive separately. The announced plan was midnight Mass, then the traditional breakfast at my older brother's house. The next morning, my sister informed me in front of our mother that she had seen my friend Pete at Mass. My mom, not particularly ignorant, immediately interrogated me as to why I would not have seen Pete as well if I had been at Mass. There were no words to deny the obvious, just a lot of ahs and ums. At this point, she delivered the "ho-ho-ho, Merry Christmas" line.

Frankly, I had stopped feeling guilty about this sort of thing. The only shame I wished to deliver was to my sister for committing such a rookie mistake. My mother would have been truly distressed if she knew what I really did during that hour. What I did was to blow a joint in a nearby parking lot, *then* went to my brother's to satiate what was by then a ravenous appetite.

This brings up the parallel set of behaviors to my fading adherence to Catholic rules: my steadily increasing drinking and pot smoking. I cannot blame this on my Catholic upbringing. My predilection for substance abuse stands apart from any religious training. In fact, if there is a relationship at all, it flows in the other direction. My all-or-nothing personality was what drove *both* my rejection of Catholic legalisms *and* my substance abuse. I was not wired up to accept a middle ground or a moderate temperament.

The spiritual effects of this fading adherence would come later, and not without another significant attempt to square the Catholic theological circle. The effects of my partying, however, began to manifest themselves much sooner. It's not that my grades suffered because of my partying. In fact, as I rolled into my junior and senior year, my grades went up. This is primarily because I was taking courses that interested me, which many of the required core classes did not.

My drinking, and my substance abuse was primarily drinking, had not yet cost me much, but it would. Like many such things, it started off innocuously enough—some beers at a party, a joint being passed around, nothing too heavy duty. I graduated from a few beers to my own six-pack, then to my own twelve pack, and from sharing a joint to rolling my own from my own stash.

Usage went from occasionally on the weekends to after school. Getting stoned with a good friend after school while listening to Bob Dylan's *Desire* album sticks out in my mind. The only downside was being paranoid that I would pass out in my mashed potatoes while totally stoned at dinner.

No, at that time, the cost was primarily financial—financial to my parents as they dealt with me racking up two vehicles because I was a drunk driving idiot. If it were not for the fact that the two cars I totaled were BMWs, I would not be here to talk about it. Superior German engineering and anti-crash technology allowed me to survive, as well as prevent me from killing close friends. As I said, I lived in a no-problem world.

The other financial cost to my parents was one they bore unbeknownst to them. This involved the booze I and my friends drained and the depredations to my parents' home that a series of riotous parties inflicted. Depredations such as a half ounce of pot defiling a Waterford crystal bowl of my mother's. Or the many times people slept in various rooms of the house, including my parents' bed and the unknown number of sexual liaisons that occurred throughout the large home. If an image helps, think of the party scenes in the movies *Sixteen Candles* or *Risky Business*. I could make a whole book out of just the parties I threw. Honestly, I only really remember the ones epic enough to earn names, like half-ounce night, or the Shining Party, or the St. Patrick's Day bacchanal, among others. A cosseted existence and parents who traveled a lot and who did not expect such behavior added up to a toxic mix.

As I said, the increasing drinking I did was not caused by the Catholic Church or my misunderstanding of what God was trying to tell me. Yet the growing frustration certainly fed into my desire to self-medicate myself into numbness.

I found myself increasingly angry and at odds with the insulated Catholic world I inhabited. It's not that I was going around in a day-to-day rage, but I was clearly getting more antagonistic toward a dogma that I increasingly saw as nonsensical and an application that I saw as damaging. Much of the damaging application of this legalistic dogma centered around the Jesuits, or at least the more vociferous of them.

In the immersive Catholic model, you were identified by your parish. It was usually the first piece of information you gathered when you met someone new. Some of the more strident Jesuits liked to ascribe certain traits to people simply because of what parish they came from. As it happened, my parish, St. Margaret Mary's, was in an affluent part of town and close to a major Omaha park (Memorial Park) that was a hangout for drinking and pot smoking and had a few years earlier been the scene of some anti-war protests.

This tagged those of us from St. Margaret Mary's with being "heads," as in pothead or drug head. The term may have come from the Jefferson Airplane song "White Rabbit," with its line "Feed your head." It may be doubtful that the Jesuits or lay staff knew specifically about the term, but they certainly thought that we were drug users. In any event, most of the clerics and staff thought that about those of us from St. Margaret Mary's Parish.

This was a broad-brush labeling that swept up everyone from my parish, or at least made anyone from that parish suspect. Yes, it is true that many of my friends were partyers. In fact, we got to wearing the label as a badge of honor. The labeling and ostracism that the

Jesuits employed did solidify our group of close friends, if only to stand against a common enemy.

This did result in a grand moment: the fall pep rally in my sophomore year when I had made the varsity cross-country team. The non-football sports team got one moment in the spotlight by being introduced before the school. When my name was called, my friends immediately began to shout "Cleary, smoke pot!" Truth is, it warmed my heart to stick it to what I considered to be a bunch of judgmental jerks. I am not denying ownership of my partying, but by being branded an outlaw by the Jesuits, it certainly made it easier to justify my behavior based upon an "us vs. them" grounds.

This broad-brush labeling also swept into suspicion many, if not most of the boys from my home parish, who had nothing to do with heavy drinking, let alone pot smoking. It also ignored the number of top academic and athletic performers from St. Margaret Mary's. It also ignored the fact that kids can and will try things they ought not to as a part of adolescence without it making them ax murderers à la *Reefer Madness*.

The whole effort to stigmatize was based in ignorance. One Jesuit claimed that he wasn't sure if it was all the money families from my parish had or our proximity to Memorial Park (as if substance use did not occur in *any* other city park) that made our parish population "sit in our basements with rock and roll blasting loud and smoking our pot." Again, I am not creative enough to make up this kind of ignorance.

The effects of this stigmatization were real and damaging. It created a gang-like atmosphere between us heads and what we called reds, as in redneck. This resulted in some actual fistfights and an unnecessary level of tension that divided our class. All of this was impossible to square with the love we were supposed to show one another as followers of Christ.

That we were ignoring the religious instruction that was being delivered to us was clear by the way we approached our annual religious retreats. Freshman retreat was as a whole class in the gymnasium, so there was little opportunity for shenanigans. Sophomore through senior year, however, were in groups of about twenty. These retreats were mandated as part of the curriculum and took place outside of town at a specially designed retreat center. Today I would relish the opportunity to get away and explore my faith in a bucolic setting over the course of a weekend, but at the time, it was only another in a lengthy list of religious *obligations.*

My friends and I took great pains to make sure we went on our retreats together and craftily dodged the Jesuits' attempts to keep us separated. They were a drunk fest and nothing more. We hid booze in our 1970s era tube socks and made sure to have a good supply of weed. One year, one in our group drank so much that he barfed in the barracks. In junior year, one of my good friends came late because of a varsity basketball game. He arrived totally stoned, telling the Jesuit in charge that he was not the boss of him. Anyone but a clueless Jesuit could see that he was one baked boy. For senior year retreat, we all voted for a contemplative approach with quiet walks around the grounds. We did this so that we could meet at the bottom of a hill and get stoned. Obviously, floating on a cloud of pot does not bring one closer to Jesus, but we really could not have cared less.

Getting more aggressive than passive

It might be tempting to think that this anger and apathy directed at the Jesuits was generated in retrospect, but that would be inaccurate, and I have proof. My anger and angst reached a crescendo at the end of my junior year. This came pouring forth in the form of my responses to a questionnaire handed out by the yearbook staff and moderators at my high school. They wanted feedback and quotes for the yearbook, and at that moment, I was ready to give it to them. I am not sure why I was so angry, but it is evident that I was. I distinctly remember being in the back of the class (heads always sit in the back, duh) and furiously writing out my responses. It was not really the right forum for this kind of rant, but it was the only such opportunity I ever had while at this institution. This is what I wrote at that time.

I have inserted a scan of the original as proof. A legible copy follows, the only edits being spelling corrections.

To: All Seniors
From: The Yearbook Staff and Moderators

We would like to include quotes from seniors in this year's book. We would like to include a mixture of the witty, the clever, the imaginative, the creative, the poetic, and the profound.

Please answer any, several, or all of the following questions with whatever response strikes your fancy. Please return this questionnaire to your English teacher tomorrow.

1. As a senior, my impression of Prep is... That there is light at the end of The Tunnel. It has been a long, dark, dank, and dismal 4 years. But it is almost over. I sigh with relief.

2. Life at Prep is... Basically it is boring. It is repititious. It is not that different than any other school. But some how Prep magnifies this boredom.

3. I will always remember... Walking out the door after graduating and never looking back. I will never forget being able to make it Through Prep.

4. My best experience was... Graduation. Even Though it has not happened yet I guarentee That it will be the most memorable time in my 4 years.

5. My worst experience was... Freshman retreat. I sat in the gym, cold, and tired. Meanwhile There were a bunch of morons Spilling Their guts to the world. It was terrible

6. I came to Prep because... I really had no choice. I may or may not have wanted to come here 4 years ago. However, The main reason I came to Prep was That my Father wanted me to come

7. Anything else you want to say?... Prep has given me an education, and a pretty good one at that. However, Prep has failed to live up to its potential. The reason is simple: The Jesuits. They are hypocrts. They preach one thing and practice another Thing. These people are supposed to be men of God. Yet they are greedy, as can be evidenced by the teacher salary negotiations. They also engage in stereotyping, prejudice, and overall backstabbing. These are the very — your

Please Sign X _Thomas C. Cloney_

(Your signature gives the Yearbook Staff permission to print any portion of your above remarks.)

Things that we as christians are not supposed to do. The biggest crime that the Jesuits have committed is that they have stifled individuality. They try to force you to give up your desires for the overall good of Prep. This fails because if the individual does not grow Prep cannot grow. If this trend continues Prep will become a sterile, stagnate enviornment, which in many ways has already happened.

All this is not to say that I have been unhappy for 4 years. But the good times have not come through Prep. It has come through outside people and places. Any personnel advance ment that has happened to me has come about because of an opposite reaction to Prep. In a way Prep helped me because I saw in Prep everything that I did not want to be and then tried to become the exact opposite.

Overall Prep faces serious problems. If the exodus of teachers continues Prep will become a poor school. If the Jesuits continue their bad ways Prep will become a shell. I was lucky I saw through the B.S. and avoided being trapped by Prep. But how many more innocent people will fall into the "Prepway" without ever seeing another alternative. Unless Prep faces up to the fact that it has serious difficulties, it will continue to slide and become a neomort.

neomort — an organism whose brain is dead but whose other organs function normally.

To: ALL Seniors
From: The Yearbook Staff and Moderators

We would like to include quotes from seniors in this year's book. We would like to include a mixture of the witty, the clever, the imaginative, the creative, the poetic, and the profound.

Please answer any, several, or all of the following questions with whatever response strikes your fancy. Please return this questionnaire to your English teacher tomorrow.

1. As a senior, my impression of Prep is…"That there is light at the end of the tunnel. It has been a long dark, dank, and dismal 4 years. But it is almost over. I sigh with relief."
2. Life at Prep is…"Basically it is boring. It is repetitious. It is not that different than any other school. But somehow Prep magnifies this boredom."
3. I will always remember…"Walking out the door after graduating and never looking back. I will never forget being able to make it through Prep."
4. My best experience was…"Graduation. Even though it has not happened yet, I guarantee that it will be the most memorable time in my 4 years."
5. My worst experience was…"Freshman retreat. I sat in the gym, cold and tired. Meanwhile, there were a bunch of morons spilling their guts to the world. It was terrible."
6. I came to Prep because…"I really had no choice. I may or may not have wanted to come here 4 years ago. However, the main reason I came to Prep was that my father wanted me to come."
7. Anything else you want to say? "Prep has given me an education, and a pretty good one at that. However, Prep has failed to live up to its potential. The reason is simple: The Jesuits. They are hypocrites. They preach one thing and practice another thing. These people are supposed to be men of God. Yet they are greedy as can be evidenced by the

teacher salary negotiations. They also engage in stereotyping, prejudice, and overall backstabbing. These are the very things that we as Christians are not supposed to do. The biggest crime that the Jesuits have committed is that they have stifled individuality. They try to force you to give up your desires for the overall good of Prep. This fails because if the individual does not grow, Prep cannot grow. If this trend continues, Prep will become a sterile, stagnate environment, which in many ways has already happened.

All this is not to say that I have been unhappy for 4 years. But the good times have not come through Prep. It has come through outside people and places. Any personal advancement that has happened to me has come about because of an opposite reaction to Prep. In a way, Prep helped me because I saw in Prep everything that I did not want to be and then tried to become the exact opposite.

Overall Prep faces serious problems. If the exodus of teachers continues, Prep will become a poor school. If the Jesuits continue their bad ways, Prep will become a shell. I was lucky I saw through the B.S. and avoided being trapped by Prep. But how many more innocent people will fall into the "Prep Way" without ever seeing another alternative? Unless Prep faces up to the fact that it has serious difficulties, it will slide and become a neomort*.

*neomort—an organism whose brain is dead but whose other organs function normally."

Whew! Wow! That is some angry rhetoric. In retrospect, I was more than a little ungracious. Jesuits are people too, and as such, they are as fallible as the rest of us. Clerics possess all the same human foibles as the rest of us, and now I am not nearly as harsh. I can clearly see as well that I was painting with too broad a brush. There were many fine Jesuits living out their gospel call as best they humanly could. In my defense, I was seventeen years old. However, much of what I wrote then remains, to my mind, accurate.

It was startling to read that I was condemning the things the Jesuits did as being "things we as Christians are not supposed to do." I was self-identifying as a Christian, notably not a Catholic but a Christian. I was grappling with the cognitive dissonance that would so bedevil me later.

I would also hold my comments about steamrolling the individual as being essentially correct. Yes, we live in a community and society. Yet unless the individual is cared for and allowed their freedom, the larger group cannot succeed. This is true in small groups, businesses, congregations, and larger societies. You cannot have a group before you have one. Add to this the fact that our relationship with God is uniquely individual and is meaningless without our freedom to say no. All of this marks the makings of a spiritual crisis. Looking back, I can see the Lutheran in me struggling to be let out.

The main point is that I was looking at the world through the lens of works righteousness that my entire experience with the Catholic world had given me. As someone young and idealistic, it was not surprising that I looked upon a failure to live up to an impossible God standard of works as hypocrisy. One of the first things someone in this type of situation does is to look outward and condemn. It becomes much more spiritually damaging and dangerous when you turn that idealistic lens upon yourself. That would be several years away.

While I was wrong about Prep failing (it is still there after forty years and apparently doing well), I was right about not really looking back once I left. I briefly attended only part of two reunions until my more recent forty-year reunion. I went to this one because I have become convicted of the idea that regardless of my experience with the institution run by the Jesuits, I have a history with my classmates, and those early relationships matter. Besides, I was also wrong in that many of my classmates turned out well despite the Jesuits.

I have, however, not given a dime to Omaha Creighton Prep and am not at all a "Prep Man." In a conversation at a work dinner many years later, I met a woman who discovered that I was a Prep grad. She immediately asked what I thought of Prep's new president. I paused, then explained that I was vaguely aware that Prep had a new president because I saw a headline in the local paper, but that I was not at all an active alumnus. It was then that I fully realized that Prep in fact had no hold on me. That and the whole being a Protestant thing.

To close the loop on this story, I forgot all about this questionnaire over the summer. That summer, my group of friends and I mellowed. We had one year to go, and we had made good friendships, and it took too much energy to maintain that level of anger. Even the conflict with the reds cooled. Most of the reds began to drink beer and even smoke some pot, and they did not turn into ax murderers, so they mellowed as well.

At the beginning of my senior year, the Jesuit who headed the counseling department caught up with me in the hallway. "I read what you wrote," he said. *Crap*, I thought, *I'm cooked now*. Father then said that he would put himself down as my counselor that year so that "if there was anything I did not want to talk about, I could not talk about it with him." He then handed me the questionnaire, for which I am now so grateful, and then he let me go on my way. As I said, there were good men in the Jesuits.

The remainder of senior year was a relative cakewalk after that. I had given up cross-country, with only a minimum of tension over that fact with my parents. I was then free to take elective classes I liked and did well in. I was also free to concentrate on partying all the way to the finish line. As for my relationship with the Jesuits, I reacted as citizens late in the Soviet Union must have responded to communist propaganda—treating their pronouncements as empty words wasted on one who was no longer listening and who no longer cared.

4

Worshipping the Bottle

Becoming the drunk I was meant to be

So after graduating from high school in 1981, wanting never to look back at this Jesuit institution after all my passive-aggressive pushback, after my legally signed rant against the Jesuits, where did I enroll for college? A Jesuit university, of course. As I said, never underestimate the power of cultural Catholicism.

It is not as if I had to stay in a Jesuit educational setting. My parents were well-off enough that I could attend any university that would accept me. They imposed no requirement to go to a Catholic or, specifically, a Jesuit university. The only restriction that was placed upon me was that my inquiry should not be so broad as to include Boston University. This was because my brother attended there in the early 1970s, and my parents were certain that this was the reason he turned into a long-haired hippie.

So I thought about where I wanted to go and applied at the University of San Francisco. There were no college tours the way there are today, even among the well-off. I picked the University of San Francisco because I had been to San Francisco, and it was an amazing town. Who wouldn't want to party there? Also, two of my sisters had gone to Lone Mountain College by 1981, a part of the University of San Francisco. Another sister had gone to USF for her freshman year, so I had some familiarity with the university itself.

Also, a good friend from my high school class was going as were two members of one of the Catholic all-girls schools in Omaha, whom we hung out with.

So I got admitted, set up in their system, packed what I needed, and boarded a plane going to the Bay. All courtesy of Mom and Dad's credit card, of course. I don't remember much after that.

That is not literally true, of course, but it was closer than a non-drunken person would ever think. I was on my own, except for paying my own bills. There was no curfew. There was no one telling me I had to be anywhere specific. There was no one making demands of my time. This is a step toward adulthood. This is a bit of practice for real life. Most parents want this for their children, and most children want to be free of these kinds of restrictions. They want to be the boss of themselves and think that they are ready for it. I certainly thought I was ready for it. I was ready to be unshackled and given my freedom. So I had my measure of freedom. What I did with this freedom was to faceplant in a drunken pool of my own creation.

The only thing that was unshackled was my incipient alcoholism. During this full academic year, I blossomed as a raging, out-of-control drunk. People will often ask "were you a bad drunk?" "No," I usually respond, "I was a stellar drunk." It was one of the few things that I was naturally good at. I fully blossomed as one outstanding, drunken fool.

One of the first things I did was join a fraternity. There were only two on campus (USF was small anyway, with about 3,500 undergraduates). I was panicked into not having a social group like the one I had in high school. It never occurred to me that my high school friends were years in the making. No, I wanted instant friends, and fraternities offered this. What they also offered was a consistent stream of drinking occasions.

This may sound a bit strange to any millennials reading this, but alcohol was ridiculously easy to acquire in 1981. One of the first things one of my fraternity brothers did was to take a group of us across the Bay to Oakland to get fake identifications. I gave them my Omaha address but Portland, Oregon, instead of Omaha, Nebraska. They gave me a picture ID that had a disclaimer at the bottom of the document to protect them from legal liability. This disclaimer was easily cut off and voila, I had a drinking passport. Few people checked identification in those days, and when they did, they easily overlooked the obvious fakery.

Our main spot to get package booze was just down the street from the dorms. The official name of the establishment was Fulton Foods, as it was on Fulton Street. It was known on campus as Filthy Foods, as it was a dump. The rule of thumb was *never* to buy anything but prepackaged foods from Filthy. Notably, this rule did not apply across the street at Dirty Donuts. Filthy never asked for an ID, and all he cared about was that whatever booze you bought was carried out in a brown paper bag. Cheap booze, illegally but easily obtained, a short walk from a college campus, what could go wrong?

What could go wrong was obvious, and it went wrong almost immediately. I did not just drink regularly; I was drunk five out of seven days. I don't mean that I was past the legal standard for intoxication. I mean I was blotto five out of every seven days. My schedule was very regular, especially for a drunk.

Monday was fraternity meeting night. The frat house was a short walk from campus, and there was a liquor store on the way. In the first semester, I bought a quart of beer for the meeting, and second semester I was buying two. After the meeting, we went to O'Rourke's Bar, a hard-core Irish pub. Hard-core as in posters of Margaret Thatcher Wanted for Murder and very pro-IRA posters. Here we would drink until uproariously drunk every Monday.

On Tuesday, I took off but started right back up again on Wednesdays. That was floor drinking night of the second floor of Gilson Hall. A floor buddy of mine, also about as drunken a fool as me, and I would listen to *The Hitchhikers' Guide to the Galaxy* on the local NPR radio station while getting totally ripped. We would, of course, keep drinking long after the radio program and usually bouncing about the dorms and causing trouble (more on that in just a bit).

Thursday was campus bar night. Yes, in 1981 there was a university-owned and operated bar on campus, the *Fog and Grog*. One of my fraternity brothers introduced me to one of the key bartenders, and from then on, when she was working (and that was a lot), she let me drink for free. Because this was repeated over and over, this bar lost three hundred dollars per week that first semester. A bar on campus, in an era that did not take underage drinking seriously, managed to lose itself three hundred dollars per week. These were Reagan dollars, mind you. Three hundred dollars was not chump change in 1981. Sadly, at the semester break, they fired everyone and got new management, so we had to start paying for our debauchery.

Anyway, Thursday was band night at the *Fog and Grog*, so off we went with our fake IDs. What followed was a loud drunken time that saw us come back very loudly to the dorm, only when the bar shut down. Friday saw me back at the *Fog and Grog* at noon, wearing my favorite hideously loud 150 percent polyester drinking shirt. Friends and acquaintances came and went during the afternoon as I got numbingly drunk. I would stagger back to the dorm sometime after 6:00 p.m., after pulling a good six-hour drinking shift. I would pass out soon after.

Saturday was date night for those not such drunks as to be able to carry a relationship. Not being one of those, I would hang out in the dorm and drink, usually from room to room. In another aspect of a bygone era, dorm rooms were treated like domiciles at this time. Therefore, neither the resident assistant nor any university official could just walk into your dorm to curtail illegal activities. This was true even if the door was open. The only place they could enforce any order was the floor lounge, although they rarely did even this. Once again, I would pass out at some point.

Sunday was the other day I took off. This was mostly from sheer exhaustion. I would sleep until 10:00 or 11:00 a.m., then stagger to brunch and spend the afternoon watching football or reading the Sunday paper. This pattern repeated itself for most of my freshman year.

The cost of this drunken outburst

It is difficult to tally up the cost of all this, either financial, emotional or in terms of relationships, or of my dignity. Financially, I was constantly broke and in debt. I borrowed incessantly from my roommate. He was a vet, so he had a stipend from his stint in the army. He also was ROTC, so he got money for books and incidentals. This made him a wealthy man by college standards. He became my bank.

Also, one of my financiers was a fraternity brother who also happened to be one of the two pot dealers on campus. He would float me a bag or two (the man dealt in quality merchandise by the way), then I would pay him back with about half of what my parents would send me. The upshot was that I was constantly short and owing somebody money.

The financial cost got even heavier by the end of the first semester. My Wednesday night second floor drinking buddy and I went on a drunken rampage one night and found, of all things, a shopping cart on the top floor of the dorm stairwell. After bouncing the cart off every wall between the eighth and the second floor, we finally got it to our floor. To this day, I honestly only thought about how cool it would be to own a shopping cart.

I still have no idea why we did what we did next. One of the elevators was out of order and stopped on the first floor. We managed to open the door from the second floor. We then proceeded to place the shopping cart as well as a plethora of trash cans (there had been a hallway bowling tournament that night, using trash cans as pins) onto the top of the broken elevator. We then went and passed out in our respective dorm rooms.

The next workday, they repaired the elevator and did a test run up to the top floor, not knowing of all the junk we had put on top. The shopping cart and other items got wedged in the gears and burned out the motor. As we had been so loud in bouncing the cart down the stairs in the first place, it did not take long for the campus authorities to apprehend us. We were sent straight to the head of operations, the true head of the university, as the Jesuit president served only to raise funds.

I tried to make a good show of it. I got a haircut and shaved, a rarity that year. I even wore a tie to the proceeding. When I walked in, the shopping cart was in the outer office, mangled and looking like a piece of modern art. I knew I was toast. The proceeding was short but merciful. My partner in crime had gone before me and pleaded to stay enrolled rather than face expulsion, which would have been customary. So I was spared expulsion. We had to pay the cost of repair, which was $1,975, $987.50 apiece. Remember, Reagan dollars. This was serious jack in 1981. The money was fronted by my good friend who had enrolled with me at USF from high school. I had enough money in my savings, but this was in an account I needed my parents' permission to access. He graciously lent me the money until the following summer when I could pay him back out of earnings from my summer job. This did, on the one hand, allow me to forever keep this incident from my parents, but on the other, took away the funds I was going to use for my second semester drinking. So I once again found myself perpetually borrowing and then scrambling to repay people I knew so that I could continue drinking. I also had to write an essay about the dangers of drinking. I remember that it wasn't half bad, but I did not believe a word of it at the time.

The emotional cost was even steeper than the financial cost. Frankly, I hated myself, and I knew it. I had zero self-esteem, and after a time, I drank to numb myself to this reality. I lied to people I called friends to get the funds to buy alcohol. I would drink half filled, warm beer leftover from a party just to keep pumping my body full of alcohol. I was overweight, slovenly, and a pig. If anyone could come close to living like Bluto in *Animal House*, I was it that year.

I began to regularly black out during my drinking escapades. There were too many of these blackout events to count. It became the rule, not the exception. There would be mornings when I would wake up not feeling particularly hungover and think "okay, I had a decent night." I would think that until the stories started coming forth about what I had done. Things like "You and a buddy came into my dorm room via an army crawl. What was up with that?" Or "You were staggering all over campus. How did you get home?" I got to where I began, proactively asking people if I had done anything drunkenly stupid the night before. It was like living the movie *Memento* every morning, only with a splitting headache.

The relationship cost was heavy as well. There was, of course, the relationships that I failed to forge. I had drinking buddies that freshman year to be sure. Whether they were friends is a more problematic question. For the most part, no lasting friendships were formed. I certainly did not form any relationships with any women. I was totally emotionally unprepared for such a thing.

My drunkenness did create strain with those relationships that I had forged that year. I distinctly remember one of my fraternity brothers being furious at me because during a drunken stupor, I let on about his liaison with someone other than his actual girlfriend. I ended up almost never seeing the two women from my high school years, being too drunk to make any such time for them. My high school classmate I did see regularly, as he joined the fraternity with me. That was unfortunate for him. Although there was no *one* thing I did, it was clear by the end of that year that the relationship would never be quite the same.

Spiritually, I might as well have been dead during this time. I never went to Mass, I certainly never prayed, and there was almost no recognition of anything greater than myself. Except for alcohol, that is. Booze was my god, and drunkenness was my worship. I regularly attended the church of the drunken idiot, and my falling repeatedly was the thing that drunks did when they prostrated themselves before their god.

In fact, the only Mass I attended my freshman year was the weekend my parents came to visit. They asked what time Mass was, and I assumed 12:00 p.m. It was in fact 12:15 p.m., and it was a High Latin Mass. This is not just Mass in Latin, but it is in fact a Latin Mass that is *sung*. This is the only such Mass that I have ever attended. That is too bad because I am sure it is quite a beautiful thing to behold, if one is not suffering a debilitating hangover. Needless to say, my lame excuses about really going to Mass in the dorm and therefore not knowing about the time or nature of this Mass were not believable to my parents.

To the extent that I was engaged at all in issues of faith or belief, I was narrow-minded, to say the least. I do remember gay rights issues coming to the forefront on campus, and I spoke approvingly of a hard line taken by some very conservative Catholics. This was more a case of simple bias than systematic belief in Catholic orthodoxy but an ugly remembrance nonetheless.

By the end of that freshman year, I was emotionally crippled, spiritually dead, and knew instinctively that I had to get out of this environment. So I gathered up the gaudy twenty-one college credit hours that I had accumulated (that I had a 2.9 GPA was testament to USF's lax academic standards) and announced my intention to transfer back to school at home in Omaha. In furtherance of the proof of the power of cultural Catholicism, I enrolled at Creighton University, a Jesuit institution.

Same bottle worship, different congregation

The transfer did not address the underlying issue of my alcohol abuse, but it did afford me less opportunities to get raging drunk. Given that I was living at home with my parents, I could not go get falling down drunk five nights a week. I had to keep my drunken rages to the weekends and/or summer days. It was even by then getting difficult to get raging drunk on back-to-back nights.

I was also closer to most of my high school friends, the majority of whom were just down the interstate in Lincoln at the University of Nebraska, so I had plenty of safe drinking space in which to seek besotted refuge. While the number of drunken occasions was reduced, the severity and costliness did not lessen. I was still careening wildly out of control, and only in retrospect did I realize that I was heading for a major life crash.

The pattern was simple. I ate when I was hungry, slept when I was tired, and drank whenever I got the chance. Gone were the massive blowout parties, which seemed a bit passé by the time I got to college. Getting drunk in bars was more the thing at this point. The college bar close to campus was one such spot. Or traveling down the road to Lincoln to hang out at the bar scene in that college town.

Still a thing was making a fool of myself repeatedly—drinking to a stupor, being loud and incoherent—like trying to play trivia in a Lincoln bar and being good at it, so good that I drunkenly shouted out the answers to all the questions even when it was not our team's turn. Then there was the deep embarrassment of passing out on top of a jukebox in a Lincoln bar while the great bluesman Magic Slim and the Teardrops were playing. Wandering out of a bar so drunk I forgot to tell the people I was with that I was leaving, on more than one occasion, was also a part of the spiral downward.

What was gone was any semblance of joy or fun. Like many things, drinking started out as fun, a good time shared with longtime friends. Parties, crazy fun, and a shared history being built up. As time went on, it got to be a weight, a source of drudgery. It was habitual because I did not know anything else and continued to self-medicate myself to numbness. Carrying the bottle forward felt like what Frodo must have felt like as he took the ring closer to Mount Doom, a heavier and heavier weight.

A teeny, tiny soapbox

To the extent I was connected to God at all, I had become a bit preachy. I had retained enough of my Catholic upbringing to insist that adhering to the rules and traditions was the only way forward. I "shared" this in a way that was not inviting, somewhat harsh and thoroughly judgmental. Of course, what I was preaching was nowhere near the way I was living. I was not even making that much of an effort at it. There were times when I would try to attend Mass regularly, adhere to some prayer discipline, and attempt to live what I thought was a Christian life. In the end, my relationship with the bottle was stronger than the one I wanted with God.

I could feel the repulsion of those I talked to about following this path, and I had by this time so thoroughly misunderstood what God was telling me that I could only demand from others the works I had been taught would save people.

I was at the same time continuing a downward spiral in my personal life. My drinking had consumed my ability to function productively in school and my GPA had cratered to a 1.7. Unfortunately for me, Creighton was far more academically challenging than the University of San Francisco, so slouching my way to a decent GPA was not an option. I was missing tons of class and turning things in late and generally acting as nothing more than a middleman for the Anheuser-Busch corporation.

All of this added up to me standing atop a very small soapbox made of weak wood and demanding that people live in a way that I could not. The lesson that we don't have to *do* things to curry favor with God was many years down the road. I had entered a vicious downward spiral of being a preachy jerk, who was living totally contrary to what I preached and who drank away his hypocrisy. The breakdown of this rickety soapbox and me with it was just around the corner.

Down and out at the Stardust Lounge

The Stardust Lounge was a strip mall bar not far geographically from where I was living with my parents. It was culturally a million miles away. It was a dark, dingy, dismal place. The drinking area was poorly lit, and the shades were always drawn. When leaving, either into the mall or out to the parking lot, your eyes were assaulted by the lighting contrast. That you are squinting due to the light outside a bar is a testament to the fact you are drinking at a time of day when most are engaged in productive activities.

This lounge was a refuge for some who wanted to not shop with their spouse. Mostly, it was a sewer for those in the grips of late-stage alcoholism. I remember the bartender was an old-looking man, bent over with gnarled fingers, their gnarliness accentuated whenever he opened a can of beer. I would call a friend who would meet me there after my college classes let out. He was useful because he was a willing drinking partner as well as someone with a car.

The drinking would start in the early afternoon, usually on a Friday. We would continue to pummel ourselves with booze until the early evening. I was usually too spent to attempt any other social activity, which was good. I mean, who wants to associate with someone that drunk anyway? The pattern was to meet my friend, place a drunken call to my mother, and then continue to drink until either our bodies or our funds gave out. While I would not describe myself as being blind drunk, I was drunk beyond the ability to reenter the house without help. I was beyond the capacity to put the key in properly and/or turn it the correct way to unlock the door. On many occasions, my mother would have to unlock the door and let me in.

Busted: The beginning of the end

This pattern continued for most of my sophomore and junior years of college. My spirits and grades sank steadily, and my behavior did as well. The beginning of the end occurred in the fall of 1983 on a Cornhusker football Saturday in Lincoln, Nebraska. I and a couple of drinking buddies drove down to Lincoln from Omaha the night before, about a forty-five-mile trip on the interstate. Yes, we were drunk and in fact went on a last-minute lark. We figured we could crash at the frat house of a good friend, so off we went. That we did not crash and burn on the way was sheer luck. We got to the frat house and partied some more and crashed.

Being enterprising drunks, we were up early and at it the next day, about 6:00 a.m. It was a game day, and this was when the Nebraska Cornhuskers were a national powerhouse. We did not have tickets but would watch on TV and, of course, get royally drunk all the while. We went out on a food run about 10:00 a.m. or so. On the way back to the frat house, I clipped a curb and immediately a cop turned on his flashers and pulled me over.

I don't recall if he gave me a field sobriety test; they are not admissible in court anyway. However, the blood alcohol content (BAC) test was. I blew a 0.19. The legal standard in Nebraska at that time was 0.10, so I was just shy of twice the legal limit. To put this in context, you need to understand how the body processes alcohol. I only found this out later during alcohol counseling. The body burns off an ounce of alcohol (about one beer or drink) per hour even while you are still consuming. For my body type, 0.19 equals about twelve beers, which was what I tested at around 11:00 a.m. that day. Since I started drinking at about 6:00 a.m., you add five beers to the total to account for the one ounce of alcohol per hour that the body burns off. Quick math: 6:00–11:00 a.m. equals five hours, so add five beers to the twelve I had in my system when I was busted, and you get around seventeen beers consumed that morning.

I was guilty as hell, and I knew it. My friends bailed me out within an hour or so, and I was given a court date. I tried, ultimately in vain, to keep the incident from my parents. I sold my album collection and anything else that might fetch a couple of bucks to pay the coming fine. I was a first offender, so I was not concerned about any jail time. In fact, the prosecution made it clear from the start that I was looking at probation and a "diversion" program. This meant that I would have to attend alcohol counseling classes, Alcoholics Anonymous meetings, and keep my record clean during the probationary period. If I did all these things, then the conviction would be "set aside" and not show on my record.

I cannot remember how my parents found out, but in retrospect, I was glad they did. It was good to have support, and my dad stood with me in the courtroom. It did not take long; I pled guilty, and the judge handed down the sentence I was expecting. The prosecution did try to make an issue of the fact that I did not pull over right away when the police turned on their sirens. I think the judge appreciated the fact that I admitted that I did do this because I was drunk, so what would you expect, quick reactions? I also remember the Mothers Against Drunk Drivers (MADD) representative in the back of the courtroom knitting away and keeping a watchful eye on the proceedings. I am just lucky I did not get busted a few years later when the anti-drunk driving environment was a good deal less hospitable. In any event, I was on my way to a post-convict future.

The weekly drunk-dry cycle

I was not really committed to being a sober person after my conviction. I was not ready to admit that I had a particular problem with alcohol. I rationalized it as I did a dumb thing and got caught. I was cognizant of the need to not drive drunk, as was my regular habit. At some level, I knew this was a dangerous idea. Also, my "set aside" was dependent on not being arrested with another DUI. If I was, the first conviction would go back on my record permanently, and I would be sentenced as a second-time offender. Even while not admitting I was an alcoholic, fear served as a pretty good motivator.

Except when it didn't. I did drive drunk a few times after my conviction. I was not obscenely drunk as in the past when I nearly killed several friends in the awful accident in my mother's BMW, but drive drunk I did. I tried to not go very far and was paranoid about it. Luckily for me, I never was busted for this.

During this time, late 1983 and early 1984, I was attending the required alcohol counseling classes at a community center in Omaha. I never went to AA and was never called on it. Once I realized I was not going to be held to account for this truancy, I figured what the hell. I was still in denial anyway, so this fit the pattern.

The counseling did plant seeds, however. They took a while to germinate, but they were important elements to recovery. I remember distinctly the counselor asking about my BAC level when I was arrested. He then had me do the math to ascertain how much booze I had consumed in total. When we arrived at the total of around seventeen beers, he announced that most people who had that much alcohol in their bodies would not be standing, much less functional enough to drive a car, albeit badly. I immediately responded that I knew a half dozen guys off the top of my head who could drink that much or more and, in fact, who would be able to drink me under the table. He said, that was the point. I needed to consider the types of people I was hanging out with. He stunned me with revelations like that. Also stunning was the idea that people at weddings for instance were not all drunk. People at parties were not drinking themselves into a stupor, and in fact, most people in the world drank socially and did not regularly get drunk. He rolled out the statistics that one drunk driving arrest meant about a 33 percent chance of having an alcohol problem, a second arrest a 66 percent chance, and a third meant you were an alcoholic. This impacted me because I knew that I could have been arrested dozens and dozens of times for driving drunk and that I had not been—complete luck.

It was starting to dawn on me in late 1983 that I might have a problem. I began a regular cycle of going to the alcohol counseling classes on Tuesday, having sworn off booze after the previous weekend. Then I would be smashed on Friday and Saturday and start the cycle all over again. Wash, rinse, and repeat. I was admitting in the alcohol counseling classes that I had a problem, and at some level, I may have believed it, but at a deeper core level, I was in denial. I thought I could control it, but my time at the aforementioned Stardust Lounge said otherwise.

Rock Bottom

Every drunk who recovers hits a rock bottom. Even drunks who don't recover hit a rock bottom, but they never realize it. Rock bottom is a thing you likely only recognize in retrospect but can sometimes realize in the moment. It was the latter for me. I knew at an instinctive level that I had hit the lowest point in my life. It all occurred during one of my forays to the Stardust Lounge. I was with my usual drinking buddy on a typical besotted Friday afternoon. I am not sure where we were planning to go after the Stardust, but I did know that I needed to alert my parents to the fact that I would not be home for dinner. I went to the pay phone (that seems so ancient now) and called home. I was so incomprehensibly drunk that I was not sure where I was or what I was doing. All I remember from the conversation was my mother telling me I *had* to come home. I had it in my mind that there was some sort of emergency. I cannot remember if I went home immediately or not and do not remember arriving home. Blackout drunk was now the norm, not the exception.

What I remember is the aftermath. My mother related what had occurred during the conversation on the phone. I had called, and my dad answered. Apparently, I did not nor could not recognize his voice. I simply did not know who I was talking to. He must have turned the phone over to my mom who then drilled it into me that I needed to come home right away. She could not believe that I could not even recognize my own father in the state I was in and how that made them feel.

I had arrived at my rock bottom. I have never felt more pain, shame, or regret for anything I had ever done in my life. The wrecked cars and strained relationships with friends were as nothing compared to this. I had inflicted a level of pain that could not be measured on the two people who unconditionally loved me and cared for me my whole life. Scumbag was too good a term for what I had become.

It was not long after that, perhaps within days, or hours, I honestly cannot recall, that I had my reckoning with the bottle. I broke down. I don't mean simply that I got emotional; that did happen. No, I mean all that I was as a human being, all that comprised my personality, all that I was or could ever at that moment hope to be, broke. I was completely deconstructed as a person. It was the most intense period of aloneness I have ever experienced. I don't mean loneliness. I have never felt that as I was always convicted that there was someone to care for me regardless (owing no doubt to my upbringing). This was different. This aloneness was just me, as if suspended in space in a universe devoid of anyone else. It was only me facing the blackness and the inescapable reality of what I had done and what I had become.

The truly scary thing is when you realize that as bad as rock bottom is, there is a bottomless abyss awaiting those who do not climb up from rock bottom. I knew that while I was at the lowest point in my life, a worse fate awaited if I continued. I knew that death was clearly in my future because of my drinking. I figured if I was lucky, I would go out alone in a solo accident very quickly. I knew, however, that the more likely scenario was to die slowly by degrees while inflicting a massive amount of pain and suffering on everyone around me. Neither option was terribly appealing.

So, alone in my room, literally in the dark, I broke. I finally and fully admitted to myself the reality that I was an alcoholic. It was not like the admissions I made during the counseling classes. This time, I believed it because there was nothing left of me but the drunk, and I knew it. I finally disgorged the demon that had control of my life. The alcohol was not the demon. The demon was my own weakness and personality. While this truth was hidden inside of me, it had control of me. In forcing this truth out of me, it became possible to fight this demon. This disgorgement that awful, fateful night of my aloneness was the closest I will ever come to knowing what it must be like to deliver a child. It was as if another being was forcibly pushed out of me. The relief I felt at arriving at this point was palpable. I knew it would not be an easy fight against that demon, but it was a fight that I could win if I kept that demon in front of me. In that moment, I chose to live.

Wagon riding and falling

So I climbed aboard the sobriety wagon. I am not sure why it's called riding a wagon, perhaps a fig leaf to America's frontier past. In any event, it is as apt an analogy as any. My first ride on the wagon lasted all of thirty days. I had an opportunity in the early spring of 1984 to spend a weekend with friends at Lake Okoboji. This is a lake in northern Iowa about three hours' drive from Omaha. Many in Omaha, including several friends' families, had vacation property on the lake. It had been the scene of some notably drunken adventures from time to time. This weekend, we were planning to stay at the city park in tents. Only in your early twenties does this sound even remotely appealing. I made it through Friday night in good shape, but by Saturday, I was blasted. Sunday brought not just a hangover but a good deal of shame.

This backsliding did not feel at all like the ones I had experienced during my weekly drunk-dry cycle. I knew instantly that I had screwed up and had been knocked on my ass by the demon. However, the demon was not in control. My acknowledgment of my underlying problem was deeper than one fall off the wagon. I also realized that I was in no way prepared for a trip to such a location as Lake Okoboji, it's existence in my world only serving as a location to drink. I would have to be smarter about the environments I put myself in, at least for the foreseeable future.

So I climbed aboard the wagon once more. This time my ride lasted three months. I was avoiding obvious drinking situations and those people in my life who, while friends, were really drinking buddies. I made it all the way to November 10, 1984. It was a Saturday. The previous Tuesday, November 6, Ronald Reagan coasted to reelection. This was a large moment in the life of a young Republican/ Libertarian, or so I thought at the time.

That week, after the election, my parents left town on a trip, so naturally I had a party to celebrate Reagan's reelection. Just as naturally, I got drunk. I remember getting into some of my parents' better wine, and then I remember waking up half under my bed next to a fair amount of vomit. In fact, the last several times I drank I got sick, a sure sign my body was reaching a breaking point in its ability to process alcohol.

Once again, the hangover/shame was real but not the same as my wash-rinse-repeat cycle. I knew that I had screwed up, but I was still in control and had not reversed the conclusion I reached that awful night of my final breakdown. I was an alcoholic, and that would never change, but I did not have to continue to be a drunk.

So I climbed atop the wagon once again. The date was November 12, 1984. I am anal enough that I counted Sunday the eleventh as a drunk day since I was drinking past midnight. Therefore, Monday the twelfth became my sober anniversary. I have ridden the wagon ever since. It does get easier, but there is not a day goes by that I do not think of that day and my need to be sober *today*. Everything in my life that I have or ever will have is made possible because of what happened on November 12, 1984. It was literally the day I poured the foundation upon which I built the rest of my life.

Was God on the wagon with me?

I was spiritually in flux during this period. I was not in any way systematically connected to my faith and was not regularly attending Mass. The church was appealing to me at some level, but frankly, I was too consumed with getting and staying sober to be in any way an observant Catholic or to give it much systematic thought. The one thing I did intentionally decide was that unlike my teeny, tiny soap-box period as an obnoxious Catholic, I would *not* preach to anyone about my sobriety or theirs. I had made a decision that applied only to me. I had to do this to live; others might not be in the same situation. I knew that if I preached, it would drive my friends away, and who could blame them? I also knew that there would be drinking buddies who would fade in my life, but by not preaching, I would be able to sort out my real friends from those with whom I only had a drinking relationship.

So perhaps in a subtle way, God was guiding me. I had learned enough by my repulsive preachy period that this sort of fundamentalist attitude was not an effective way to communicate or proclaim what you were all about. I decided that it was better to just live out who I was, that being a sober person. Those who were my friends would see that and, if truly my friends, would accept that. In the end, that is what happened. Some relationships faded, as some were clearly threatened by my sobriety and not interested in a friendship but a drinking buddy. Others, after some obvious trepidation about my new life choice, came to realize that I was the same twisted, warped SOB I had always been but without needing to peel me up off the floor. Besides, I provided an instant benefit of always being a designated driver.

As my life recentered upon my sobriety, I did begin to reengage with my faith and grapple with what it was I believed in. I would make attempts to begin a prayer discipline and commit to going to Mass regularly and *do* all the things I thought I was supposed to do. This usually occurred around religious holidays and events. It did give me the warm and fuzzies, but I found momentum hard to sustain. I do think in retrospect that God was with me during this period, and He kept me sober, and therefore alive, for a purpose. I just did not fully understand it that way at the time, and since I kept trying to *do* things to gain God's favor, I was still not understanding Him clearly. In a perverse way, my arrival at sobriety fed into my misunderstanding that things were in human control. My sobriety was in my control. I had decided to not drink and was maintaining it, not always easily, but I was gaining sober strength by the day. This likely reinforced my belief that there are works people can do to gain their salvation, earthly or otherwise. I would see where this would lead very shortly.

5

Cognitive Dissonance: Failing to Renew

In the mid-1970s, there arose a movement within the Catholic Church known as the Catholic Charismatic Renewal movement or Renewal for short. It was an attempt to reinvigorate the church and its membership by reigniting a spirit of passion for the church and her teachings. Its heyday was probably the early to mid-1980s. This is when I became involved with this group.

I was trying to connect with my faith and my heritage of Catholicism. I was seeking and trying to understand. My involvement with this movement was a part of this. A grade school classmate, who was still living in the old parish at the time, was involved with the Renewal movement and asked me to participate. I really do not remember how or why she reached out to me. I know her to this day and have always been struck by her faith and passion for the church. I find this somewhat ironic; she is such a strong feminist and believer in gender equality that she would make a wonderful Protestant. Nonetheless, she was and remains a fine Catholic in the best of that tradition.

The Renewal movement had produced a series of learning materials, some of which were designed for small group study. Much later, I would become very familiar with small group religious study, but at the time, it was all quite foreign to me. I do not remember a lot of the specifics, but it was questions for discussion that centered on trying to connect people with the church community and the wellsprings of our faith.

One reason I think that it was all foreign to me is that in the day-to-day tradition in which we were raised, we were simply told the rules and expected to obey. This was, to be fair, a bit more sophisticated than that. It did not challenge the dogmatic claim for the necessity of works, but it did not emphasize it either.

I am also not entirely clear as to the exact timeline of these small group gatherings, but I do remember it was after I had gotten sober. In any event, I approached these studies with an (for me) open mind. I do recall looking forward to the events and was genuinely desirous of connecting with my faith.

The bugaboo was, as it has always been, the concept of works. While this course of study did not emphasize it, it is impossible to be a Catholic without thinking that there are works to be performed to gain justification before God. Again, many other Protestant denominations fall into the same error, just not as formally. There is just no way around this dogma nor its real-world implications.

Those implications are dire upon deep reflection. I was *finally* moving beyond my teenage rants at other people's hypocrisy and was beginning to mature into looking in the mirror at my own shortcomings. I found those shortcomings legion. As I said, one of the ways that I kept many friendships was by not preaching about my sobriety and convincing people that I was the same twisted guy I had always been, albeit sober. In many respects, I surprised myself with this revelation. I *was* the same twisted guy, in good fun ways and in deleterious ways.

In true Catholic fashion, I viewed myself as vile and depraved. In objective terms, I was. I knew it. I was completely aware of what I was, what I felt, and what I did. I was in fact not substantively different than I was before I became sober. Yes, life is better sober than not. Life is in fact only possible for me sober. However, this did not mean you ascended some moral escalator to a higher and loftier plane of existence. Given my predilection for self-effacement as well as the emotional number the nuns had done on me, I was always prepared to view myself in the worst possible light.

I was coming face-to-face with the same problem that has afflicted millions of people before and since—reconciling your behavior with an impossibly high God standard, the standard, of course, being perfection. The most famous person so afflicted was Martin Luther, but I did not have any of his theological training. It is no wonder my reaction was quite a bit different from his.

I attended a few of the Renewal small groups study sessions, then I remember I had a scheduling conflict off and on for the next few weeks. I distinctly remember not feeling any better or worse about myself for not attending as when I did attend, so I decided to just save time and quit altogether.

This was the beginning. I began an informal process of intro-spection and based upon the standard of works righteousness I had been taught, I continued to measure myself against the God stan-dard of perfection. Not surprisingly, I failed to measure up again and again. The cognitive dissonance became too great. I could not reconcile my behavior with this standard.

Much later, I would understand that at a normal volume this dissonance is the Law speaking to us to convict us of our need for redemption, which is to be found in Jesus Christ. When the vol-ume is set to maximum, it is no longer the Law speaking to you but Satan. You hear that you are not good enough, unwanted, not possibly loved. You begin to believe you will never be worthy of God.

The answer, as I now fully understand, is faith in Jesus as Savior. Hearing and believing the good news that we are forgiven, full stop. In the world I was brought up in, yes, you had to have faith, true enough; Catholics believe in grace, but you also had to *do* works. But I knew, and I still know that we can *never* do enough works to get right with God. This was a piece of belief that is still with me today. We really cannot do anything for God to make ourselves worthy of Him. Now I understand that I only need to believe the Word, and I am saved. Then, though, I thought there were works to be per-formed, works that would never be satisfactory. The volume was on full blast at this point: *You are not, nor will you ever be, good enough!*

When you finally *hear* the gospel and understand God, then the voice is shut off, and you realize you don't have to *do* anything, simply believe. You will change *after* that *because* of your new understanding and seek to do the best works you can. The problem was, at that point in my life, I was incapable of hearing the good news and understanding God.

There are three ways you can respond to this situation. One is to simply ignore the problem and push it all to the back of your mind. This leads one to living an unexamined life, and we all know what that is worth. Apparently, so do millions of others, given how many do not choose this option.

The second option is to solve the problem. Study Scripture and the theology and figure out that this is not what God is telling us. This is what Martin Luther and the other reformers did. I had neither their courage nor their training to accomplish this, so I choose the third option.

The third option is to drift/walk/run away. Choosing this option does not really shut up the voice telling you that you are unworthy, but it does put you far enough away that you cannot hear it any longer. Also, upon reflection, I was concerned that if I continued to view myself so negatively, I would be putting my sobriety at risk. I was clearly cognizant that much of my drinking was driven by the fact that I loathed myself. Adding a level of loathing by measuring myself against an impossible God standard was too much to bear.

So that's how it ends, with a whimper not a bang. I simply drifted, I steadily allowed myself to drift farther away from the voice yelling at me about what a piece of garbage I was and got on with my life. The drift would pick up steam and turn into a walk then a run, but the falling away from my faith and the church was rather anticlimactic.

This was nothing like the breakdown that occurred prior to my arrival at sobriety. There were no tears, no emotional episodes, it was just…well, nothing. Nothing is exactly where I was headed toward. I just could not see that as the destination at that point. I was just glad that the yelling in my head about how unworthy I was, brought on by full-immersion Catholicism, was over.

6

Lost in the Wilderness

Works righteousness taken to its logical extreme

Whether you believe in God or not, you can still adhere to the theology of works righteousness. To most people, me included (at this time), it is taken as axiomatic that if you want to get right with God (if in fact He exists), then you must *do* something. Agnostics and atheists think that those who believe are trying to do something to curry God's favor. I would argue in fact, especially based upon my experience, that works righteousness can in fact lead one to a state of nonbelief, or its equivalent, what I would call functional atheism.

The entire notion of works righteousness is based on the underlying assumption that we are in control of our faith and lives, not God. Relatively, few will openly admit this, but it is logically true nonetheless. If there is something I must do to curry favor with or please God, then it puts me firmly in control. This is the appeal to humans. We forget the fundamental reality of the universe: God is God, and we are not. This error is what caused humanity's fall in the first place.

If we are in control as the logic of works righteousness demands, then if you go far enough, why do we need God at all? If we must do this or that to gain heaven, we can decide our fate. If this doctrine is real, then those who preach it are hypocrites because they fail to live up to it in relation to God's standard of perfection. If we try to live up to it, we recognize ourselves as hypocrites because we fall far short of this standard. Rather than live with this impossible standard or follow people we see egregiously failing this standard, why not exercise the control we think we have and jettison the standard altogether?

By jettisoning the standard, we throw out the baby with the bathwater. We stop trying to have any relationship with God because of the logical conclusion that we draw from this works righteousness doctrine. This does not always, or even mostly, manifest itself in outright atheism. However, it might as well. If we drift, walk, or run away from any relationship with God, He is not a part of our lives, and we remain in a broken state. But since we are "in control," we think that is all right.

This is certainly what occurred with me. I, as I often tend to do, took this logic to its inexorable conclusion. I was in control. My continued sobriety reinforced this. If I was in control, then I did not need to adhere to a standard that caused so much cognitive dissonance and feelings of failure. I had jettisoned the standard that works righteousness demanded. It was only a matter of time before I put myself in total control and jettisoned God completely.

During this time, I had completed my undergraduate degree, started and lasted two weeks in law school, then worked part-time at a corner drugstore. Started and left a graduate program in history (my undergraduate degree). For someone who thought he was in control, I appeared to be drifting aimlessly. The only real positive was that I was remaining sober. All I knew is that even if I ended up as a ditchdigger, I would be a sober ditchdigger.

Intellectually, I was grappling quite strenuously with what I believed politically. I was trying to systematize and rationalize my beliefs into a coherent whole. I read and read and organized what I thought about various topics and certainly got in touch with my classical liberal/libertarian self. I was growing increasingly laissez-faire in my domestic beliefs and more and more a rationalist in my philosophical beliefs. This latter phenomenon was all a part of being "in control." Since I was drifting aimlessly at this point, I certainly had plenty of time to indulge this activity. Chalk another one up to patient parents who provided a no-problem world.

This intellectual path culminated in the summer of 1988 when I attended, courtesy of parental funds, the *Cato Institute Summer Seminar in Political Economy* at Dartmouth University. Overall, it was a terrific experience. I was exposed to some fine thinkers in the classical liberal tradition who expounded on the benefits of a free society and limited government from a variety of perspectives. I still have the notes I took from these lectures and still find them valuable.

However, I was also exposed, for the first time really, to people who were actively atheist, especially an intellectual named George H. Smith. George H. Smith is a noted libertarian and atheist. He has written for over four decades on these and related topics. He was at this seminar to discuss the philosophical underpinnings of modern libertarian thought. He did a most admirable job of it. It was in the after-hours conversations, which are an important facet of such a conference, that I became aware of his strident atheism. He was not rude or personally disparaging of believers, but he was very open and confident in his nonbelief. He certainly seemed in control of his life, and he was most in control of his thought.

This interaction piqued my interest, and after my return home, I checked out Mr. Smith's most famous work, *Atheism: The Case Against God.*[1] As I read, it fed into my notions of control, reinforced by my past experiences with works righteousness as well as my by then four-year-old sober journey. I was in control, in my mind at least, and the case Mr. Smith made appealed to me.

It was an extreme defense of rationalism and reason as *the* only way to secure knowledge in this universe. This in the mind of Mr. Smith precluded belief in a higher being. As he argued, "It is not my purpose to convert people to atheism…(but to) demonstrate that the belief in God is irrational to the point of absurdity. If a person wishes to continue believing in a god, that is his prerogative, but he can no longer excuse his belief in the name of reason and moral necessity."[2] One key reason Smith holds this view is his claim that the natural world is the only world there is, and reason is therefore the only tool to knowledge. However, Smith cannot make this statement if he does not know the totality of the natural world. In short, Smith so narrowly defines what is knowable as to disallow the existence of a God.

Smith also fails to deal with the argument from logic of "sufficient causation"[3] that postulates the existence of a God as a creator and likely a sustainer of creation.

I came to understand these criticisms much later. At the time, this argument made sense to me. It appealed to my rationalist instincts and my desire for a philosophically coherent whole. It also oddly, as I pointed out, was an extension of a belief in works righteousness and our ability to be in control. I bought into this argument hook, line, and sinker. I was now openly an atheist. Being in control of oneself and being responsible for one's works had driven me to this "logical" conclusion. Never mind that I had for the entirety of my life misunderstood what God was telling me and all of humanity for that matter.

Cocooned in ignorance

In the fall of 1988, having false-started several times on deciding what career path to take, I needed to get a job and move out of my parents' house. So I took a gig tending bar at a family-owned pub and grill. The family was one I had known for a long time, one of whose members went to a local Catholic girl's school and graduated the same year as me. Of course, they were a Catholic family. Not obnoxiously so, but serious Catholics nonetheless. The owner was a successful attorney and always wanted a good, old-fashioned Irish bar to gather with his friends and family. So even in a state of active disbelief, I ended up still very much ensconced in the Catholic world. This was going to be a temporary gig, just a way to bring in some income and allow me to move out of my folks' place. I figured about six months or so and I would have something "real" to move into. This "temporary" gig lasted seven years. Not that I would have used (or even knew) a biblical analogy back then, but they were seven fat years.

It is easy to get sucked into the bar life, even as a sober person. In fact, I could not have lasted even a month if I were still drinking. I cynically decided that I could serve society best by separating drunks from their money. More seriously, the experience helped me stay sober. First, most people in a bar are not falling down drunk, despite what many may think. Second, those who were that drunk allowed me to see what I had been and never wanted to be again. It made me realize that all I was really giving up was the one to two drinks in an evening that would qualify me as being a social drinker. Breaking it down that way and seeing those who were stumblebums helped keep me focused on my sobriety.

I must fully admit that I had a good time tending bar. Not being a naturally social person, working in this environment allowed me to see people on a regular basis. I was paid to throw and attend a party. This was especially true since I knew the family that owned the establishment well and therefore knew most of the people whom they knew. Omaha, being a big small town, I ended up making a living serving what was my natural contact base.

Getting drawn into the bar life, especially when you are only planning a short stay, happens slowly. You pick up a shift, maybe two. You realize the money is good and criminally easy to earn. So you pick up another shift, then another. Pretty soon you have four shifts per week, and you have enough money coming in to move out, which is what I did. Within a month of working there, I was handed a key and asked to close the nights I was working. As it turned out, the owner's daughter who was managing and who had hired me needed someone to take on some management tasks, beyond just locking up at night. So she and I and a good friend who was working there sat down after close one weeknight and carved up the shifts and the tasks. I had four good evening shifts and was ordering the inventory and scheduling the night staff. Just like that, I was full-time in the bar world.

It was a good world for a twentysomething to be in in the early 1990s. The money was good; I was able to move out and not take any help from my parents. I was able to get some material things around me on my own terms and with my own resources. I had a good working environment and was paid to learn about business. Later I would joke that during these years, I earned my MBA (Master of Bar Administration).

It was no joke. I was graciously allowed by the owners to learn about inventory control, profit and loss experience, and most importantly, how to manage people. It is not that I never made mistakes. I certainly did, but truth be told, I was *good* at this. The family member who ran the place was amazing at getting people through the door, and in fact, the whole family had a tremendous sense of hospitality. I added the anal-retentive attributes necessary to help keep more of the money that came in.

I was able to rationalize the schedule. Honestly, this helped me make more money as a tipped bartender as well as a manager. I put order to the inventory control and the pricing. I learned how to evaluate costs and keep them lean. Most importantly, I learned how to build a staff and manage them successfully. That last part was easy. It was a popular bar at a time when the baby boomers were young enough to fill pubs and then some. The contact base of the owners was upscale, solidly upper middle class, with a lot of young professionals. In large part, the client base was graduates of my high school and the corresponding girl's schools that the Catholic Church ran. Additionally, the local university, my alma mater Creighton University provided a good number of customers. All these groups also provided a steady stream of people who wanted to work at a fun hopping place like this. I never had to recruit or search for employees; they came to me in numbers greater than I could accommodate. These were almost all good people from good families who were trustworthy and who could helpfully bring their friends along with them as customers. The staff was our marketing tool. So I was able to settle into a fun, profitable, and practically useful occupation. Life was good.

Life was also small. Not that there is anything wrong with any of this, but my world was tiny. I was living in a small yet very comfortable bubble. As indicated above, this bubble was way too small for God. I spent the first couple of years of my unbelief shocking people at parties by self-identifying as an atheist, but this got boring quickly. After a time, I only discussed it if it came up, which was not often. There seemed little reason to go down that road when I was too busy showing others a good time and being overpaid for the privilege.

My world was literally small. I mean, geographically small. I was living a couple of miles away from the bar. I could walk if my car was in the shop. The auto shop was down the street, the owner being a regular. The grocery store was down the block, the laundromat was within a mile. Almost every service I needed was within a two to three square mile radius of the bar. This was true except for the short time I lived in a more suburban apartment.

My routine, and I remained a creature of the routine, was simple. Get up around noon, eat, and get dressed. Run any errands in the afternoon and be in to work by 5:00 p.m. The bars closed at 1:00 a.m. in those days, so I would get out of there after cleanup by 2:00 a.m. most nights. Busier nights took longer to clean up, and with a larger staff, we might hang out, throw darts, and get takeout. I would then usually stop for junk food on the way home. Arriving home, I would watch television, read the news, and eat, crashing about 5:00 a.m. Then start the whole thing over again. Often on Fridays, after a usually busy Thursday shift, I would lie in bed watching daytime television and snacking until it was time to get ready for work. Soon this routine was so set in place that there was no time made to look for "real" work. I did not want too anyway.

In my off-hours, I began to spend more time around the bar. I would often go in after the lunch rush, get fed, and hang out with the amiable day drinkers. On nights I was not working, I often ended up with a "busman's holiday" by hanging out at the bar with my friends since that is where they wanted to go. Or I would hang out at the bars of other friends who were also in the trade. Sundays doing this was a particularly fond memory.

While it is true that most people in a bar are not smashingly drunk, there are moral compromises one must make to work in this trade. The reality is that you serve people who then get into cars and drive drunk. You serve people you know are cheating on their spouse. You serve people you know are circling the alcoholism drain. You break up fights and clean up puke. I am not naive about the downsides to this. I worked it four to five times per week. However, overall, it was a good world populated by good people.

This was a happy little world I had stumbled into. It was really the only world I cared about. I used to be just a short-time prior, someone who cared deeply about what was going on in the world. I kept up on the news of the day and engaged intellectually with that world. This seemed like the thing to do as a human being and as a person of faith. While I still read the local paper and maintained a subscription to the *Wall Street Journal*, it mattered very little to me. I peered at the outside world primarily through the television at the bar. Peering was about all I did. The bar was patronized by professionals, and the Nebraska Medical Center was close by, which brought a fair number of doctors and med students in as customers. This fact made for above-average bar conversations, but they were just superficial conversations. It is never good bar business to argue vociferously with patrons, but truth is I did not care too anyway.

I barely remember the Berlin Wall falling in 1989. One of the most momentous occasions in the twentieth century and all I remember was serving someone a beer as I glanced up at the television. The first Gulf War does stick out. I recall being somewhat offended at patrons partying it up on an otherwise quiet night. I also remember a bar employee, a college kid who worked as a doorman, overdosing on the first day of the war. He came barreling in, strung out on caffeine, unshaven, having stayed awake for the first twenty-four hours of the conflict. He was ranting about how the Iraqis had stolen all the incubators from Kuwait. To which I replied, "Yes, and the Germans cut off the right arm off every Belgian youth in 1914, except they didn't." As an aside, this spurious claim made by the H. W. Bush administration was as much a lie as the 1914 propaganda put out by the British. However, the fact remains that this was a one-off event. I simply did not care much about world events. I have a greater memory of Mike Tyson losing to Buster Douglas while on vacation in Hawaii in 1990 than of anything important happening on the world stage. One of the long-term knocks about Christians, and people of faith in general, is that they are too focused on the next world to care enough about this world. The ironic fact of the matter is that I never cared so little for this world as when I did not believe in the next.

It's not that I was critical of people who believed in the next world. Much like my decision to not preach to people about my sobriety, I was not inclined to preach to people about my unbelief. I was not out to convert anyone to atheism, nor was I intent on ridiculing people for their beliefs. Most of my friends were still believers, if only nominally. I suspect that many were functional atheists but not willing to take the formal step that I did. Being a member of a large Catholic family, I would find myself in church. Weddings, funerals, and other occasions brought me across the threshold of many a church. I never thought it appropriate to disrespect others in their houses of worship. So at least I can look back and state with accuracy that I was not an overtly obnoxious atheist.

First stirrings of discontent

The first stirrings of discontent were not religious or spiritual but relational. I had always assumed that I would end up married with children, and that prospect was appealing. A bar *seemed* an ideal place to meet a woman and develop a relationship. While there were certainly opportunities, a bar as a source of a relationship was problematic for a sober person. By the time you get to know a woman well enough to ask her out, you realize that she probably spends too much time in a bar. I had several relationships with women like this. Good, intelligent women, yet in the end, too much the partyers. That is not to say that they stayed that way. I came to realize that most people went through a period in their lives where they partied and drank too much. Most people go on to grow out of it. As I went along in the bar world, I "graduated" many customers to establishments that catered to older clientele or to a life as a married person. I was needing to find someone on the way to a more sedate lifestyle.

After a series of uneventful relationships and dates, I let it go for a while and did not actively date. However, by 1992, I was longing for companionship. So in true analytical, I'm-in-charge-of-things fashion, I decided that one of my goals in 1992 would be to date more. To that end, I did secure dates with more promising women than the excessive drinkers who had previously disappointed. Not much came out of these relationships, yet I was not discouraged even as the year dragged on. It was then that fate seemly intervened. I certainly was not a believer in fate at this point in my life. I am not so much of one even now. I just don't think that is the way God works. It did seem though, in retrospect, that this was preordained.

In early 1992, I was in a car accident on the way to work. It was not my fault; a guy about my age took an ill-advised left turn in front of me and totaled my car. No one was injured, just property damage. This led me to needing a new vehicle. I ended up with a 1981 BMW 7 series sedan. It was in cherry condition, and I got it from a bar patron and paid in cash. Literally cash, as I paid for most things in those days.

It was now early December, and I was driving along in my cherry BMW and was distracted enough that I rear-ended another car. Again, no one injured, just property damage. My car was undrivable. Since I had paid cash and since I did not want the notably higher premium that came along with complete auto insurance coverage, I only had liability insurance on my cherry ride. This meant that I had to pay for any repairs out of my own pocket. Fortunately, I found a guy who could rebuild it with used parts and do it reasonably cheap. Cheap enough that I could afford it and not care that it took him almost two years to complete the job.

Because of *this*, I needed extra money. As it was coming up on the holiday season, I asked the manager (part of the owning family) if I could pick up shifts at the relatively new banquet room they had built across the parking lot from the bar. She graciously said yes, so I was set to work some holiday parties.

One of the parties was for a law firm whose attorneys were regulars of the bar, especially the partner organizing that year's event. He wanted me at their party, and I readily agreed. While at the party, I noticed an attractive redhead and mentioned that to the owner. Passing comment, so I thought.

The next week, I was working another party for another law firm, and the owner told me the redhead's name and that she was expecting me to call for a date. I protested that I was sure she did not know who I was and was told that no, she knew me from the bar. So I spent a few days working up the courage to call, and I finally did so. She agreed to a date, and we went out January 2, 1993.

By August, we were living together, and by Thanksgiving we were engaged, and we eloped to Hawaii and were married January 20, 1994. All of this because a bad driver turned in front of my car the previous spring. I think it was the philosopher Ferris Bueller who observed that "life moves pretty fast." Yes, it does, and while it may not have been "fate" the way most people (including me) understand the term, it was a momentous development and spun my life in an entirely different and genuinely fateful direction.

As a brief digression, 1992 was also significant for another reason. It saw me reengage with the newer music of Bob Dylan for the first time since he converted to Christianity. His first religious album, *Slow Train Coming*, was released in 1979. I saw Dylan perform live in January of 1980, in support of that album. In fact, he only played music off that album, none of his old standards. It was after that that I drifted away from all his eighties new releases. In retrospect, they held no interest for me because I was in a world of nonbelief. This was the period of his overtly religious era, and I was just not interested.

I continued to listen to his older music, but that was it. I did not see him live until September of 1992. I had run a side party at the reception hall next door to the bar where I worked, owned by the same family. It was a success, and I was flush with cash. As it happened, Dylan was performing just after Labor Day that year, and I rented a limo and bought six tickets and invited five friends to join. One friend turned me down, and I don't really blame him. Dylan was fresh off a disastrous appearance on the Letterman show. It was a train wreck. He was likely wasted and verbally incomprehensible. Nonetheless, I rolled the dice and went to the show. It was amazing. He was in good form, enthusiastic, and very comprehensible. He played a mix of old and new, secular and religious, all with a tight band behind him. Much of it was totally new to me. I began to realize that there was a tranche of Dylan music that I was not exposed to, and I was frankly getting bored with listening only to his older stuff. So I began to reengage with Dylan's eighties output, ending my irresponsible cultural apostasy of ignoring any Dylan work. This reengagement, over the next several years, would turn out to be critically important in my journey back.

I spent the first year and a half of my married life working at the bar. It was a different way of living to be sure. It was not so easy to extricate myself from the "life" as I might have wished. The money was good, and finding something I was interested in was not as forthcoming as I might have wished. I figured that a sales job would be a good fit, but without actual sales experience, it was hard to get callbacks. So we went along for that first ten months seeing each other when I had a night off and for passing moments during the day. I would say, because of the enduring nature of the marriage, this arrangement did not hurt us and may have helped. It was like slowly dipping your toe into the water rather than jumping in all at once. It got us both more slowly used to the compromises that are necessary for any successful relationship. However, it still sucked to not be living a "normal" life together.

As 1994 rolled into 1995, I became more intentional about finding a path out of the bar world. This became even more urgent when we discovered that we were expecting our first child. So I took the right-now opportunity and not necessarily the right opportunity. I agreed to work for Perkins, a restaurant chain, as a general manager. It was 100 percent awful. It was working from 6:00 a.m. to 8:00 to 9:00 p.m. and dealing with a staff you had to beg to work rather than one that self-presented, as at the bar. Yes, I was in training to become a general manager of a unit, but this was a manager in name only. There was little, if any, discretion allowed in this position, and you ended up being a glorified babysitter and clerk. The only positive thing about it was that it got me out of the nighttime bar life.

Fortunately, the bar life had given me some contacts, one of whom was a former coworker who was now selling this restaurant chain coffee on behalf of the Sara Lee Corporation. He was leaving this position and let me know about it and put in a good word for me. Long story short, I got the job selling coffee off a boxy route truck and had my first "real" career job. I was on my way to a normal life as a married family man, albeit one who still did not believe in anything greater than myself or this world.

The importance of the bar years

I know that it sounds odd to stress the importance of working at a corner bar, but it is all about the power of community. What the corner bar offers at its best is shelter from the storm. It is a place where people can gather, where you are known, and where you are welcome. It is a place of enduring relationships. Where I worked, I have met and known some of the most wonderful people in my life. Many of them remain friends to this day. Even the ones I have not kept in contact with over the years have a special place in my heart and always will.

It is in such a place that you will find people with not just names but nicknames. It would be like the bar intro scene in *Goodfellas*. You would meet the Screamer, Tiger, the Toenail, the Ice Man, Uncle Jack, and be called upon by folks like Molson Joe and Shimmie. Even the perpetually cranky old guy at the bar had a nickname: Happy. You could look forward to visits from the Tuesday basketball team, and there were always the old guys playing pitch in the corner. If you were a regular or an employee, you were a part of something larger than yourself, and you always had a place to hang your hat. One of the greatest compliments I ever received was from a young woman who was a regular who told me one day that ours was the only bar she would go into alone, without planning to meet anyone. She was comfortable doing this because at least she knew all of us behind the bar.

Then there was the regular who was a vacation "countdowner"; he could tell you to the minute when his next vacation was scheduled. One day, after returning from a trip, he plopped down his pictures from the trip he just finished and had me look at them. It struck me that I saw this guy more frequently and knew more about his day-to-day life than some members of his extended family or good friends. It never left me how important it was to honor those relationships and to sustain them.

From that time on, I looked upon the bartender-patron relationship much like that of a doctor-patient or lawyer-client. The better analogy is that of a priest-penitent (little known fact: bartenders have the authority to marry patrons, but only for that night). Seriously, the point is that you were entrusted with things about people that *mattered* to them; you saw things that were *important* in their lives.

Even outsiders understood the power of this community, like the night Stan and Jim rolled in from Memphis on a road trip and were so taken by the community and how it reminded them of their own corner bar that they bought the house two rounds of pitchers of beer (that was how we discovered that we possessed thirty-three pitchers). You literally cannot make this stuff up.

Yes, I certainly saw my share of grotesque behavior. There were occasionally fights, one between a group of lawyers arguing about who made more money (sadly true!). I also saw people commit every excremental act the human body can commit, on one notable occasion, a woman who committed them all within a five-minute time span (note that these stories are memorable because they are rare). Yet I also saw people meet their life partners in that place. I saw people celebrate great moments in their lives and gather to heal one another at life's difficult moments. Where else but in such a community would a regular loan his bartender (me) the belt off his pants because I had forgotten mine in my rush to get ready for a first date with a young woman (hand to God, a true story). I was even honored to be asked to say a few words at a gathering of the friends of a regular who sadly died way too soon.

I saw history through and with this community (even though I was not paying too much attention). I saw the Berlin Wall fall in this place. I saw the first Gulf War erupt there. I was behind the bar and witnessed the surreal display of a bar full of patrons mesmerized by OJ's slow-moving white Bronco rolling down a California highway. I witnessed a million other events, global and local, all in the company of friends. The point of all this is that what happens in these places is *real.* This is where people really live and where they work, play, hurt, and heal. It is a shared experience that cannot be replicated, and it most certainly cannot be discounted.

Lest anyone think this is just nostalgia for my lost youth, I would beg to differ. First, I recognize my bar days are long behind me, except for lunches, eating the greatest pub grub on the planet. In any event, I doubt I could make it up even late enough until there is three hours to go until there is an hour to go (if you ever worked in a bar, you will get that). But even though those nights are behind me, they were formative. This was true for me personally, as an employee and as a patron. I experienced deeply meaningful moments via my corner bar, and still do. I, as I pointed out above, met my now wife through this bar, we went there the night we were engaged, I went there after the birth of both my children, I went there on September 11. Whether I was happy, sad, angry, or scared, I knew that I did not have to be any of those things alone. This was a place of welcome and comfort that afforded me real community. I am richer by far for that community, and I am forever grateful to all who made it possible.

My only regret is that I did not fully understand the importance of this place or these years until later. In retrospect, I see now the crucial importance that this community played in my life and my journey back to a God-given faith. This was a community that sustained me, cared for me, and loved me, and did so without condition. I was a part of something greater than myself and this, unbeknownst to me at the time, laid the foundation for a return to an even greater community.

7

Thunder from God's Distant Shore

My wife: The pillar of my life

As with all things, faith is in God's hands. It was God that brought me back out of the wilderness, and it is God that sustains me in faith. However, God works on earth through the people that He puts in our lives and the circumstances we find ourselves in. In my case, there were two large factors in bringing me out of the wilderness and two ancillary factors.

The largest factor was my wife. To say that she was and is the most important gift God ever gave me is to voice a massive under-statement. There is nothing more I could ask for in a partner than what she possesses. She is smart, number one in her law school class. She is beautiful, kind, patient, and faithful. She and I became best friends almost from the beginning. We only knew each other for a year before we married, but our intimacy was deeper than that relatively short amount of time would indicate. My sister-in-law, along with my brother who lived in Hawaii (where we were mar-ried), observed that she would have thought we knew each other a lot longer than we had. So true!

It all just seemed so natural. Even though she was a believer, she never counted that against me. This was a refreshing attitude for me, given my background. We always engaged each other intellectually, and that was absolutely part of the attraction. Over time, I think we both moved each other toward the better elements of each other's views and ideas. I became more empathetic and gained a broader perspective on life from my relationship with her.

Then there is the fact that she brought into the world two of the most amazing people I have ever met, our children. To be a partner with her in raising up two incredible people and to share a life in common with all of them is beyond my ability to describe. Her love and care of all of us is a hallmark to God's grace flowing through His believers.

The most amazing thing I can say about her is that she allowed me to be me, and she still does. She has borne my foibles and faults and patiently suffered my shortcomings, and she continues to do so with more grace and love than anyone on earth could or should expect. It is undeniably true that God works through humans on earth. That being the case, it is equally undeniable that He was speaking very clearly to me through this most amazing woman.

It would take time, however. Initially, I was not clear on what I was hearing, just that it was attractive and soul-penetrating. That it took time for me to understand what God was saying to me through my marriage did not deter my wife from drawing me out of the wilderness by way of her example and gifts of love and grace. She would likely deny all of this and deny that it was all planned out by her in advance. Whether it was intentional or conscious or not, I have zero doubt that God sent her to me to pull me out of the wilderness and give to me something infinitely better than a life of nihilism.

As to the specifics, she was a lifelong Lutheran from a small town. Her mom made sure she and her siblings were active in their faith. Like many people so raised, Protestant or Catholic, by the time she got to her twenties, faith had taken a back seat. It is not that she ever fell into disbelief, but many young people simply are not anchored to an active faith life or faith community. She fell into that oft repeated pattern of people in that age group.

For most believers, you come out of that funk when you get married, and especially when you have children. Many want a church wedding, and that puts them in contact with a faith community, often the community of their youth. From there you may drift again until the kids come along. In our case, we eloped to Hawaii and were married by a congregationalist minister on the beach at sunset. So it was a religious ceremony but not one that would bring you back into a community that would help sustain you.

After the wedding, and especially after I left the night life of the bar world, we settled into a young married couple's pattern. We went from an apartment to a house, and our first child arrived. It is at this point that a faithful person feels the pull to getting reconnected. You immediately wish to get your child baptized. Even though I was not a believer, I had no objection. It was understood from the beginning that she would raise the children in a religious setting, and I figured if they were not browbeat and given a variety of perspectives, I would be comfortable with all of this.

So my wife settled on the neighborhood Lutheran church right across the street from our new house, and we had our daughter baptized there. It was around this time that she formally joined this congregation. I remember because there was a new member ceremony whereby the congregation welcomed new members. I distinctly recall standing in a reception line next to her as members of the congregation passed by. In my mind, they were all "Hi! Welcome to the church" to her and all "hello" to me with a glare that said, "you are going to hell." It was most unwelcoming, even if I was exaggerating the vibe. In that church's defense, their pastor came to visit in the hospital while my infant son was there with RSV. He offered a genuine prayer and blessing, and I do remember thinking that at a minimum, he was a good man for taking the time to do so.

There was not a lot of continuing involvement with this church after the baptism. Most churches don't start formal instruction for a few years after that. My wife may have gone to church from time to time, but my memory of that is not strong, so I doubt it was terribly consistent.

We were still living at this same house when our second child was born, and he too was baptized at this same church. We had begun to realize that with the addition of a second child, it would be optimal to move into a larger house.

Apparently, geography is destiny. Our new house was far enough away from our old one that it made sense to find a new church. Besides, as the kids got older, they would need religious instruction, and the former church skewed quite a bit older and did not have a robust youth program, so my wife set about church shopping.

The very idea of church shopping was totally alien to me. In the Catholic world, your church was determined by your address. The city was divided into parishes, and wherever you were on the map was where you went to church and school. It was not until the mid-1980s, as my parents' generation reached retirement age, that the church lightened up on allowing people to keep their member-ships in the traditional parishes as they moved into retirement abodes that were in a different part of town. I just assumed that everyone followed these types of rules.

In Protestant land, however, you got to choose. My wife vis-ited several churches within reasonable proximity to our new home. They were all Lutheran churches that were a part of the Evangelical Lutheran Church in America (ELCA), which was the denomination she grew up in. The church she settled on was crucial and reflected the graceful spirit that animated her life.

Rejoice!

The church she chose was Rejoice! Lutheran Church. It was a short ten-minute drive from our home and was settled in a suburban Omaha area. At the time, it was growing very rapidly, with a lot of younger families who had a lot of young children. The church build-ing had just been renovated, and it was a new, modern, and a func-tional physical plant that could accommodate a variety of activities. It was more modern than the Gothic church of my youth yet still had a most churchlike quality to it, which struck me from the beginning. Notable was the fact that the first three rows of pews had kneelers in them. This is notable because there is no point in the Lutheran service when the congregation is asked to kneel. These kneelers were installed at the request of the senior pastor because he thought that since there were so many former Catholics joining the church, it would raise their comfort level by seeing kneelers.

The kids were old enough now to be involved in a variety of church activities and programs. The most notable was Sunday school and the Vacation Bible Camp in summer. Both concepts were alien to me, as religious instruction was daily in Catholic schools, and there was no Vacation Bible Camp. I had never even heard the term before.

The importance of all of this was that I found myself in church when the children had a "share a song" (another term I had never heard before) or the Christmas program. Also, there were times in the summer when I would need to pick up the kids from Vacation Bible Camp. It just seemed important to my wife that I attend these special occasions, so it never occurred to me to object. So I encountered this church and its staff and several of the youth ministries that my children were a part of. The vibe could not have been more different from the one I received at the former church.

I was greeted warmly, welcomed every time I came there, and there was never any negativity directed my way because I was not a member nor any judgmental feel to my interactions. This did not immediately turn me into a believer, but it did soften my view of religious people. The most amazing thing was that none of it seemed rules-bound. You just showed up, and you were welcomed. Over time, this has an impact. God was using these people to spread His word, and I was hearing a little bit more clearly.

Overseeing this amazing band of proclaimers was Pastor Ken Wittrock. Kenneth Wittrock was ordained in the early 1980s. He was brought up and educated old-school Lutheran. He probably thought he would go through life known as the Right Reverend Wittrock but instead graciously allowed himself to be known simply as Pastor Ken.

About the same time as this, I, as I stated previously, was standing atop a very small soapbox as a preachy Catholic. By the late eighties when I began my formal period of disbelief, Pastor Ken was, due to an awful vehicular accident that took the life of his senior pastor, thrust into a leadership role, perhaps sooner than he expected. In this role, he began to build a ministry and a church family. He did so with a vision of what a church should be, what a church could be, and in the fullness of time, what a church would be. What he built was nothing short of extraordinary. A place was created that was filled with amazingly talented people (that Ken selected). This place became a place of invitation and welcome, marked by outstanding preaching and teaching, passionate ministry that provided for all ages, from cradle to grave. As a result, this church grew, as all churches will, if done correctly. In time, it became one of the largest Lutheran congregations in the area.

My path intersected with Pastor Ken's by way of picking up the kids from Sunday school or Bible Camp or listening to them sing in church. Slowly the warmth of spiritual welcome worked upon me and melted the last of my resistance to my return to the cross. Bluntly, other than my wife, no one had a greater impact on that journey than Pastor Ken and maybe only one other who has had as much impact on keeping me in the fold.

I am getting ahead of myself, not that there is a spoiler as to how this story ends. Suffice it to say that the ministry that Pastor Ken built was more instrumental in speaking to me what God wants all of us to hear than anything I had experienced in my life up to that point.

Dylan Redux

One of the ancillary factors speaking the good news to me was the religious music of Bob Dylan. During the mid to late nineties, I was tired and bored of listening to Dylan's classic music from the sixties and seventies. After I saw him in 1992, I began to discover his religious output from the 1980s. I had ignored this tranche of Dylan's work, not so much out of angry intentionality but sheer apathy due to my disbelief.

I began by relistening to his first openly religious work *Slow Train Coming*, which I had purchased when it was released. From there I began to work my way through his body of religious music. Some of it was stunningly beautiful and deeply personal. Even in my disbelief, I could see that. In all honesty, it was uneven in its quality, but there were treasures he wrote during this period. Mostly for me, it was *new.* I had all new-to-me Dylan music to feast on. I certainly did not set out to get religion with this; I was just looking for something different and fresh.

Unbeknownst to me was that this music would, over the next several years, seep into my subconscious and work on my psyche. The constant stream of religious imagery and poetry cannot but have an effect over time. I sensed that it was heartfelt and genuine, even if I had no clue about the biblical references Dylan was using. I must admit that it was speaking to me, as I suspect Dylan intended this music to. He was proclaiming his faith openly and boldly. This boldness was not lost on me either, as he faced implacable hostility from the nonbelieving gatekeepers of the music world. In fact, when I bought *Slow Train Coming* in 1979, the clerk bitterly told me as he handed me the album that I would not have to go to church on Sunday after listening to this. Dylan's courage left an imprint. This was just another means of God communicating His word to me. My hearing was getting better.

Really, the pope as exemplar?

It would seem strange after all I have written about the shortcomings of Catholic theology and practice as well as its practitioners to hold up John Paul II as a factor in my return to the cross. Yet it is undeniable. Differences in theology aside, I have many serious issues with the pontificate of John Paul II. This is not the space to air out those grievances. In any event, I was not viewing his entire body of work but one, albeit memorable, aspect of it.

In the spring of 2000, John Paul II traveled to the Middle East. This was notable. The only other pope to visit the Holy Land was Paul VI, and that was in 1964. It was thirty-six years later and over twenty years since he became pope that John Paul II traveled there. By this time, he was almost eighty and in declining health. Twenty-two years as pope with a more active ministry than almost anyone previously had taken its toll on the man. I distinctly remember being so impressed with the faith of this man to go at this point in his life and make this pilgrimage.

A pilgrimage was what it was. Yes, he went to visit the leaders of the Jewish faith tradition as well as leaders of Israel, but what he really went to do was to make a pilgrimage to the place that for all Christians represents the beginning of it all. It was impressive, to say the least, to witness this hunched over old man walking along the Via Dolorosa (Latin for Sorrowful Way), the path many think Jesus walked on His way to His death. It was a study in faith and perseverance for this man, who had seen and been a part of so much modern history, to humbly journey to the wellsprings of his faith.

Equally moving was the image of John Paul II standing at the Western Wall of the ancient temple and placing his prayer there along with all the other pilgrims who had come before.

Regardless of what I thought before seeing these images and the positions I have taken regarding this man's pontificate later, these images left an indelible mark on me and hastened the melting away of my nonbelieving outer self. God was communicating through this man, and I was beginning to hear a bit more clearly.

These, then, are the four means of communication that God employed to get me to hear Him more clearly: my wife, Pastor Ken Wittrock and his ministry at Rejoice! Lutheran Church, the openly religious music of Bob Dylan, and the Holy Land travel of John Paul II. Each in their own way told me something that I now believe God wanted me to hear, namely that there was a different path than the one I had traveled, there was a different message than the one I had heard or more precisely misheard. Either God was speaking more clearly to me, and/or I was hearing more clearly. Either way, the ground beneath my wilderness path was giving way.

Sure, Jesus was a good guy, but...

One distinct stage I passed through on my way out of the wilderness was the Jesus-was-a-good-guy...but stage. This is the way a lot of people think about Jesus. It is hard to deny the power of Jesus's uncompromising message of peace and universal love. Jesus as representative of a better path for humanity is embraced by many, even open atheists. I arrived at this place in due course. It is, for many who come out of unbelief, a way station or rest stop on your journey. It was for me.

I had long since given up caring to shock people by declaring my unbelief, and I was always cognizant of being respectful in worship spaces and during religious ceremonies. This deference to those who believed was amplified by my wife involving me in a tangential way in our children's religious upbringing. Coming to church from time to time and being exposed to gracious welcoming people tends to take the edge off an anti-religious attitude.

In hearing sermons and messages during the times I came to church, I began to think about the message of Jesus. It was impossible to argue with the notion that the world would be a better place if we all lived as Jesus taught us to live. However, I explicitly drew the line at the notion that this was the Son of God and that Jesus rose from the grave. That was at the time going a bit too far. Still, that I was even engaging with the ideas of Jesus of Nazareth was a far cry from where I had been.

My faith in unbelief springs a leak

By this time, it was 2001. I was happy, working in a job I mostly enjoyed. It did necessitate quite a bit of travel, but it was travel that I could, for the most part, control. I never needed to miss any important family events, and things were going well. We were making good money, saving plenty, and were living the good life. Despite my softening attitude to religion generally and Jesus especially, I was genuinely not searching to return to the church and proclaim any faith.

What finally moved me forward on the path out of the wilderness was something more personal. In short, I had a health panic attack. I can hear the naysayers saying, "Oh, you thought you were going to die and ran to a made-up being for comfort!" Well, not exactly.

I had swollen glands and a sore throat around this same time in 2001. Most of these cases are nothing more than an infection. My doctor told me he would put me on a course of treatment with antibiotics. That would most likely clear up the problem. If it did not, then he would order a biopsy to see if it was something more serious. The "B" in biopsy is right next to the "C" of cancer, and a massive wave of paranoia swept over me. I was certain that I had a dread disease and that this was it. To this day, I cannot really say why I felt this way. Later I would understand that I tend to catastrophize events and assume the worst possible outcome.

What ensued was a terribly despairing, emotionally draining several days, waiting to see if the antibiotics would work, or if I would get the biopsy. I told no one and shouldered the burden alone, an amazingly stupid thing to do. As a result, I was hideous to be around during this time. This includes an ill-advised trip to an audience participation play, *Tony n' Tina's Wedding*, with some good friends. My foul mood and my still distaste for audience participation sank everyone at our table that night. It is still discussed twenty years later. In the end, the antibiotics worked, and I was fine. Yet the experience jolted me into grappling with some of life's bigger questions. Yet no, I did not go running into church as a scared penitent.

What the jolt did was to get me to answer some of the more eternal questions, you know, just in case I *did* die. The first, most basic question I posed was "Is there a God?" That I was even posing this was a testament to how far I had traveled due to those aforementioned ways that God was communicating to me. So I dusted off some of my college philosophy books and got about thinking about the God question.

Long story short, I was steadily moving to the notion that there was a God due to the logic of what is known philosophically as the Principle of Sufficient Causation. It made sense to me and was in its own way a retort to the work of George H. Smith and his atheist tome that had so influenced me. That said, holding a position of the existence of *a* God is not at all the same thing as believing in the God of Abraham, Isaac, and Jacob, much less in God, the Father of Jesus Christ. Yet it was a massive breakthrough. I was hearing a great deal more clearly at this point.

Then 9/11 hit. I can hear the unbelievers again, "Oh, you got religion after a tragedy, how cliché!" No, in fact, I did not. I remember the day distinctly. About two weeks prior, I had read that Dylan had a new album dropping on September 11, which was a Tuesday, when all new releases hit the stores. So my plan was to do some paperwork in my office at home, then about 10:30 or so go pick up the CD and head to my favorite eatery, my former employer.

It was my habit then to have the network morning infotainment shows on, off to the side in my home office. Out of the corner of my eye, I saw the story come on that the first building of the Trade Towers had been hit by a plane. My first thought was "Why don't more plane crashes happen in cities?" I immediately just figured the law of averages had caught up with the airline industry. Then I saw the second plane slam into the other Trade Tower, and I knew this was intentional. I cannot add anything to what all who lived through it felt. It was a gutting, heart-sinking feeling of despair. I still got the Dylan album and went to my corner bar because to not would be to let the terrorists win. Mostly, though, I went to be among a community to which I belonged.

I know that this terrorist attack drove many to church, many for the first time in a long time. Bruce Springsteen released *The Rising* in response to the event or "Reborn in the USA" as it colloquially became known. It seemed the cusp of a religious revival. It is not an uncommon response to this kind of awfulness. People seek solace in the familiar, and the churches were certainly a familiar place to many, even if they had not crossed a church threshold in decades. In the long run, it did not put much of a dent in the continuing slide in church engagement in the United States. It certainly gave me pause but did not move me immediately back to the faith. I never move that quickly regarding momentous life changes.

The remainder of 2001 saw me let the idea of God marinate in my head, and I began to think and, upon reflection later, hear much more than simply about the philosophical notion of a God. My hardened heart was softening, and I could now see that I was not long for the wilderness of unbelief.

In the clearing of faith

In early 2002, I had arrived full circle. I had to finally admit to myself that I was a believer. It was anticlimactic in a way. There was no stunning moment when I shouted halleluiah. There was no being struck blind à la Paul nee Saul on the road to Damascus. It was a simple act of putting on a cross on a necklace under my shirt. No major outward sign of this renewed faith. God knew, and so did I; that was all there was to that.

The question did arise momentarily as to how that faith would be expressed. I, especially considering the impression made by John Paul II's Holy Land visit, had to pause to ask myself if I was still Catholic. This is the power of cultural Catholicism that I spoke of earlier. After all that I had experienced, all that I had said and written about the Catholics I knew, and considered such hypocrites, I still had a moment when I thought that might be where and how I should express my faith.

It was, fortunately, just a moment. I say fortunately not because I had then or now a particular animosity toward Catholics; I do not. I had certainly mellowed and was and still am willing to draw upon the best of that tradition in my life. I recognized then that, at the very least, I owed my baptismal salvation to the Catholic faith and the Catholic parents who so christened me.

It was fortunate because to embrace that tradition again would be to embrace the works righteousness that goes along with it. This puts at risk all that I had gained from my journey back to the cross. To be in thrall to a godly standard of perfection would be to hear the voice of the devil yelling once again at me about how unworthy I was. It would be to suffer all the damaging effects of this erroneous misunderstanding of what God is telling us. The clarity of communication about this came from God via my wife. The conversation that I had with her about going back into the Catholic church and perhaps insisting that the children follow so instantly upset her in a way I have rarely seen that I knew immediately that this was not the path. I heard God perfectly in that moment. I was a Lutheran, and that was all there was to it. That I was not under works any longer but was saved by the faith that God had given me would be a clearer understanding of God's word that I would grasp in the years ahead. Suffice it to say that once again I owed so much of my eternal relationship with God to the gift He gave me of my marriage.

It was Easter of 2002 that I made my first appearance at Rejoice! Lutheran Church as a believer. I was clear of the wilderness, just not clear of the obstacles that imperfect people can stumble over, as I would discover. However, I would never again be tempted into falling for works righteousness nor thinking that the church was bound up in an org chart. It was a naturally congregating community of believers that would sustain me in many of the same ways my corner bar community had sustained me but in profoundly more important ways.

You see, as my wife was leading me to the ministry of Rejoice! built by Pastor Ken, my heart found the nourishment of faith that it sought, my mind received greater understanding, and roots were sunk deep into fertile soil, roots so strong that no wind could uproot. Here, under this man's tutelage, I was finally able to let go of that which I could not keep and firmly grasp hold of that which I could not lose. For this I will be *literally* eternally grateful. Rejoice! became for me En Gedi, an oasis of faith in a desert of unbelief, a place where I would be continually renewed and strengthened, all because Pastor Ken was visionary enough to create a place that would welcome even a spiritually thirsty wretch who had spent far too much time in that desert. He did so without hesitation, reservation, or condition. Simply amazing!

Not too long after this return, I was coming home from church, and I heard on a CD I was playing a live version of Bob Dylan's "Knockin' on Heaven's Door." This is a song Dylan frequently changes the lyrics to. Today he will sing, "Knockin' on heaven's door, just like I have so many times before." In this live version from 1975, Dylan sings "mama I can hear God's thunder roar, coming down from God's distant shore." In that moment, much of my experience became clear to me. It was God calling to me from His distant shore through the people he had put in my life. At first, I did not understand but moved a bit closer to try and hear more clearly. This process kept on—God's thunder, my moving a bit closer to hear more clearly—until the day when I was close enough to fully hear the thunder and know where and from whom it was coming. It was at that moment I realized "Oh, it's you, Lord." That it was God that called to me rather than vice versa was evidenced not long after my "outing" myself as a believer. One of my sisters was in town, and the topic came up, and she said, "Oh, I heard you found God." I, without hesitation, replied, "No, God found me." Indeed, He had, and I was now home. I would discover that staying home would require continually listening to what God was telling me.

8

Getting Bolted to the Floor

The wonderful non-process of becoming a Lutheran

I had been attending worship service (I still at times almost say "Mass") for several months when I figured it was time to formally join the congregation. I wondered what sort of procedure was involved. I laugh now because I remember later driving past a Catholic church, and there was a large sign that said "Coming back to the church? A process for you." The "process" of joining Rejoice! Lutheran Church was to attend a New Member Class. This amounted to 1) being given a tour of the facilities, 2) getting a review of some of the things that you could get involved in at the church, and 3) sitting down for a Q and A with the senior pastor. As a parting gift, they gave you a copy of Martin Luther's *Small Catechism*. I mean, it was truly small. It was 3.5 inches by 5 inches and all of thirty-two pages. It contained Luther's commentary on the Ten Commandments, the Creed, and the Lord's Prayer and his thoughts on a few other topics. There was not a rule book in sight.

The next week at service, the membership director introduced those of us joining the congregation, the pastor said a brief blessing over us, the congregation applauded, and that as they say was that. I am quite sure that if I had not gone through even this minimal process, I would have been welcomed as a full member of the church. Now the question became what to do as a new member.

Getting really involved

The fall of 2002 saw the church host a ministry fair. There were tables set up by representatives of the main ministry opportunities at the church. This was a fair number, reflecting that the congregation was almost three thousand strong. I went from table to table, picking up pamphlets and talking with the participants and getting their pitches. Remember, I am an all-or-nothing guy, and I was all in.

The first thing I realized was that I needed to take advantage of all educational opportunities. Lucky for me, Pastor Ken ran a Wednesday night study, except when there was Advent or Lenten services and during the summer. I, as a learner by nature, saw this as a chance to absorb what this whole Lutheran thing was all about.

Wednesday nights became a special time and place in the years that followed. It was, as Pastor Ken said, upper-level theology class. We undertook everything from heartfelt ways of prayer to advanced studies of Scripture and theology. Ken presented some of the best, brightest, and most challenging work from a Lutheran perspective. His ability to make it accessible and understandable was extraordinary. I learned how the Old Testament was put together. I was introduced to the theology of the gospel and to what the good news really meant. I was like a thirsty man fresh from the desert, which in fact I was.

The first thing I did to get educated was to buy my own Bible. So I went to the local Christian bookstore to get a Bible. As I was poking around the Bible section, a store employee, sensing I needed help, asked me what I was looking for. "A Bible," I responded. "What kind of Bible?" he asked. "The one that Lutherans used," I said in bewilderment. I mean, I had no idea there were different types and translations of the Bible. In fact, comically, I did not even realize until I became Lutheran that the readings on Sunday were *from Scripture.* Sure, I had heard them say a reading from the "Epistle of Paul," but it *never* registered where this epistle originated.

Well, the nice clerk at the store fixed me up with the New Revised Standard Version (NRSV) edition of the Bible, which is indeed the version used by the *Evangelical Lutheran Church in America* (ELCA), the denomination to which I now belonged. It was a simple, sturdy black pew Bible, which I still read from every day. I am also glad to say I have a variety of different translations in addition to the NRSV. It is truly fascinating and insightful to view the various translations that have been passed down throughout history.

The first thing I did with this new Bible was to begin to read it cover to cover. I downloaded a guide that set forth daily readings so that in a year's time, you would have the book completed. I got impatient and finished it in six months. In a positive vein, I wanted to be able to read the whole book through at least once; it seemed the least I could do by way of study. In a snarkier vein, I wanted to respond to people who sneered "have *you* read the book cover to cover" by saying *"Yes, I have. Have you!"* When you do read it and consistently study it, the Bible makes you a great deal humbler than that snarky response.

Pastor Ken once, during a Wednesday night class, commented that he was just beginning to get this "Bible thing." I was immediately horrified. I mean, if one of the brightest people I had ever met, who spent a great deal of time studying and speaking on this book, was just now getting it after almost forty years, what hope was there for me to learn anything from it? After a time, though, I came to realize this was a cool thing. There would never be a time when I could not learn something from this most important document. I would always be able to study it fruitfully for the rest of my life, and indeed, that is what has and will continue to occur. That said, the most important thing Pastor Ken taught me about the Bible is that it is not itself the good news; it is the thing into which the good news has been placed. The good news remains that "He has risen, He has risen indeed, hallelujah!" That is, we should worship God, not the Bible.

The great medieval Jewish scholar Moses Maimonides made a wonderful point when he said that if you take a cursory look at Scripture, you will see a beautiful silver bowl. However, if you take the time to discover what is inside the silver bowl, you will find golden apples. I have been digging golden apples out of that silver bowl ever since. It became a most loved ministry to read the Word of God from this book at Sunday service, an opportunity I am still grateful for.

I also got involved with the men's ministry, the *Men in Mission*. This was a group of good men but in the end a bit too conservative for my taste. The long-term benefit was being placed in a Tuesday morning men's Bible study, which twenty years later, I still am a member.

My wife and I participated in a Habitat for Humanity build and reaffirmed that we are not very handy. Fortunately, we found other ways to participate, including, in time, a stint for both of us on church council, including a tour of duty as president of the council. What we realized is that church employees are human beings. They have an interoffice dynamic, not always positive. They have turf battles and pursue agendas, as do employees in secular offices. This at first blush would seem to take the bloom off the rose as far as church people are concerned. In fact, it is just the opposite. It was a great practical example of how unnecessary it is to be perfect, especially since we can't. Church people can and do effect great ministry even while carrying all the baggage that the rest of us do. It is impressive to see how they help others all while dealing with their own all too human struggles. This kind of ministry work is important but not as satisfying as actually delivering help to people who need it. Fortunately, I was listening when God spoke clearly to me about this.

Sometimes the voice of God sounds just like Miss Sue

Early in my time as a member of the congregation, as I said, we volunteered for a Habitat for Humanity build. In doing so, you receive a T-shirt with the names of the coalition of churches that were participating in that build. One of the organizers told me that our T-shirts were in Miss Sue's office at church. Miss Sue was the head of the children's ministry at the church. She was one of those who were most welcoming to me when I was picking up the kids from Bible camp or Sunday school. I distinctly remember picking up the kids from camp and all the children would surround this woman in the fellowship hall and sing and pray, and she would, of course, be in tears, for she is a crier extraordinaire as well as a prayer warrior par excellence. She has continued to have a large impact on my faith life.

So after service, I sought out Miss Sue to claim my T-shirt for the Habitat build. I dutifully got in line once I had found her (you always get in line when you needed to talk to Miss Sue). The man in front of me had apparently just volunteered to teach Sunday school. Miss Sue was heaping copious amounts of praise on this man, explaining how important it was for men to stand up for Jesus and for the children to see that example. She was profuse in exclaiming *thank you, thank you, thank you*!

So then it was my turn. Mind you, I was there to claim a T-shirt from her office, but I actually heard come from my mouth the words: "I guess...I...want to volunteer to teach Sunday school." That, hand to God, is how I began what would turn out to be a wonderful decade spent in the Christian Ed program at Rejoice! Lutheran Church. Seven years in the classroom and three as Miss Sue's assistant in the hall.

In retrospect, I had no clue. If I had thought about it "rationally," I would never have volunteered. I had no teaching experience, no firm grasp of the material, and even less confidence in connecting with kids. I ended up in the fifth and sixth grade classroom, with a wonderful mentor who did have experience and who patiently showed me the ropes. This got me over the hump, so to speak, and set me up for the rest of my time in this ministry. This is a great practical example of when you hear God, just believe and act. Trust in what God is telling you and go from there. Instinctively doing this turned into one of the most joyous experiences of my life. It would also lead me to the other great ministerial passion of my life.

Spirit Matters

Spirit Matters is a ministry that provides social and fellowship opportunities to adults with special needs. There are a multitude of great programs for youth with special needs, but these opportunities largely evaporate as these folks grow into their adult years, which is what makes this ministry so unique and so important. This ministry was also one of the ministries that was on the menu for the children to choose as a part of their religious education. It was the one that my daughter picked. One of the events was "Family Game Night," and as parents, we volunteered to help.

The genesis of this ministry came from the plea of a faithful father seeking something for his adult son with special needs to do as an activity. It was born of the tireless faith of an amazing woman, our youth and family minister who, upon not finding a program geared for this man's son, went and started one. It has been said there were twelve attendees at the first meeting, a bit prophetic I know, but that's the story, and I am sticking with it. Since then, it has grown to serve over 150 clients every week between October and May.

There is nothing fancy about what this ministry does; it is a simple thing done well. Essentially, we throw a party every week. Each Thursday begins in the sanctuary with praise and worship songs and prayer requests. We then adjourn to the fellowship hall for an activity. Perhaps a craft or an entertainer or a dance or most popularly, karaoke or bingo. At a fundamental level, what we are doing is inviting people to a party who are too often not invited anywhere at all. It is about giving them something to look forward to, and as Christians, we should all recognize the power of having something to look forward to.

Like all great ministry, those who serve in it receive much more than they could ever give to it. Every week we meet an amazing group of people. They absolutely love to reconnect with old friends, make new friends, and have a riotous time doing it. They hold themselves out to the world for who and what they are and accept others for who and what they are, without hesitation or condition. They do so because they are not wired to generate the pretentious BS with which the rest of us surround ourselves daily. They stand as an incredible example of how God wants us to treat one another and how to live a fully human life. I was hooked instantly.

It is through this ministry that I am so blessed to be a part of a team of some of the most incredible people who have ever raised their hand to volunteer. While our original leader has retired, our current fearless leader is one we would follow to the gates of hell because if we did, we know she would break that gate down and kick Satan's ass, which is in fact what she is leading us to do one week of Spirit Matters at a time. The darkness, hate, and death are pushed back one act of uplift at a time, one act of inclusion at a time, and one act of service at a time.

I am going to be even bolder than this and state that this is *the* most important and impactful ministry that our congregation allows us to perform. This is not to denigrate *any* other ministry. We have a large congregation and have a variety of ministries there. We are blessed with an incredible children's ministry; we have an on-site food pantry, whose reach is ever-growing. We support a Habitat for Humanity build; we have a dynamic men's group that focuses on hunger issues. We feed over four hundred families every Thanksgiving. Additionally, we have a variety of prayer, educational, and fellowship ministries. All that said, I am standing by my statement that Spirit Matters is the most important. You see, I can conceive of a world where we don't need food pantries, or Habitat builds, or other material support ministries. I can conceive of a world of rising real incomes and equitable distribution of wealth, free movement of goods, services, ideas, and people. In short, a world of peace and freedom. Now I know such a world is not soon in the offing, but I *can* conceive it. Even if such a world sprang into existence today, people with special needs would still need help. There is simply no way for them to sojourn across this vale of tears without assistance. That is why they go to the head of the line; that's just the deal. When you listen to God and understand Him, the most amazing things happen to you and through you.

Because of all these ministries and amazing, incredible people, I knew there was no going back. I was a believer; it was as simple as that. I was able to integrate rather seamlessly into this community because of my experience with community during my bar days. What had gone before was prologue for what was happening at this time. In ways too subtle to notice at the time, I had been preparing for this all along.

I found that it was true that God takes us all as we are but that He does not keep us as we are. Since I believed, I sought as best I can to do the most for those in need. I came to understand at a visceral level that we do what we do *because* God loves us. In this community, I came to understand that no matter our failings, God would continue to love me and all His children. This community reminded me of that every day, which is the whole point of being in community. All the bolts were in place now; I was not ever letting go. This does not mean, however, that you never stumble, as I was to discover, nor does that mean that I was hearing and understanding God clearly enough.

9

Turns Out You Have to Keep Listening to God

The arrogance of renewed faith

I did not intend to get arrogant about my renewed faith. I mean, who does? It did not start out that way. In fact, it started out with a rather humbling experience regarding Scripture. It was at the same time I was struggling to understand Scripture and embrace a framework for studying the Bible.

Our senior pastor led the discussion, which was constructed to evenly offer both sides of a rather contentious topic. I was excited for this study, and not for a good reason. It was my opportunity to reaffirm some exclusionary ideas I had about God's church. Even though the pastor played it straight down the middle, I was slowly persuaded by the weight of biblical evidence and the use of a crowbar upon my narrowed mind by the Holy Spirit to change my thinking on this and adopt a more welcoming stance. I did a 180 and turned completely around. In the process, I discovered a sensible way to approach Scripture that has served as a template ever since, taking the Scriptures in their full context, historical, linguistic, and literary. The point is that this was a true watershed moment; everything that came after was different from what came before.

I was feeling much more confident about my faith journey after this experience. The kind of confidence that often presages a stumble. It's not as though I was walking around disparaging others, but I was internally thinking that I "had arrived," as if faith was a destination point and not an enduring journey. It appeared I had figured out the big questions, and while I was still aware that I could learn much more, I was starting to take understanding God for granted.

The mechanics of moral compromise

I was going along well in my new faith community and learning and growing, if thinking that I "had arrived." It was never a problem for me in reconciling a life of faith with a no-problem existence. I have always understood that God *never* promised a life free from problems or struggles. I am not claiming the kind of struggles that people deep in poverty or oppression experience but human struggles there were, nonetheless.

On January 2, 2007, I began a new job. This was after having spent 1995–2005 selling coffee to restaurants and institutional users for the Sara Lee Corporation. I had then drifted somewhat until I stumbled into the financial services field. I say stumble because who when they are young says "hey, I want to be an internal wholesaler for a major insurance company when I grow up"? Life and career choices just don't work like that. Anyway, this was a fateful decision, which resulted in major moral compromise.

The mechanics of moral compromise operate a lot like the adage of "how do you boil a frog?" The answer of course is by turning up the water a little bit at a time so that the frog does not notice until it is too late to escape, and they are cooked. Working as a wholesaler in the financial services field is a lot like that. It is worth a digression into the weeds of this industry, as many find themselves in a similar situation.

This is all a bit wonkish, but please bear with me, as it is important in understanding the mistakes even the faithful can commit. Let's define our terms here. Wholesalers come in two varieties in this business: external and internal. External wholesalers live in the area in which they call and meet with advisors face-to-face. They meet individually with advisors or in groups in a branch office. They also make presentations at regional and national conferences and other such events. These individuals maintain the personal relationships with advisors and are the quarterback of the sales team. This is where the serious money is in this field.

Internal wholesalers, by contrast, usually work at a call center in a centralized location. They serve as the day-to-day contact between advisors and the company. They provide technical information, run hypothetical illustrations, prospect for new advisors to work with, as well as sending out company literature and sometimes making appointments between external wholesalers and advisors. This role is not pure sales in that internal wholesalers are not fired for lack of production whereas external wholesalers are.

Every mutual fund company and insurance carrier operating in this industry has a similar model. There may be variations such as the breadth of the product line represented and the types of advisors seen, but this outlines the dominant form this distribution model embodies.

It is important to understand the background of the people in this field. Most wholesalers, both external and internal, come from the role of a financial advisor: a failed financial advisor. It is axiomatic that if these people were successful as a field advisor working directly with clients, they would have remained in that capacity. My own experience was along this traditional path. I was never comfortable working directly with consumers as my background was all business-to-business sales, so it was not a good fit. Consequently, I was not making much money, and the handwriting was on the wall. This is how most enter the world of wholesaling.

The first thing about entering this field is the discovery that there is such a thing as wholesaling at all. When one thinks of wholesaling, one thinks of auto parts and plumbing supplies. It is hard to imagine a warehouse full of annuities and mutual funds. I found out about this niche from the individual who recruited me into the business. He knew I was struggling and suggested I go and apply at an insurance carrier that had their sales desk in my hometown.

I was only dimly aware of financial wholesaling even though I had sat in on presentations of an external wholesaler and partook in the obligatory free lunch so provided. I do remember (after becoming a wholesaler) that one of the external wholesalers who called on our office was suggested by the office manager as a good financial advisor candidate. When approached by a senior advisor in the office about such an opportunity, the wholesaler informed her that he was making over 250K as a wholesaler and saw no reason to go back to the world of prospecting widows and retirees. Eye-opening, to say the least.

I, like most, who failed as a field advisor had studied hard to acquire my securities licenses and was not ready to leave the industry without at least trying in another capacity. Besides, I was needing an income, and the first thing you learn about wholesaling is that they provide a base salary unlike being an advisor, which is straight commission.

So I investigated the opportunity and discovered that being an internal wholesaler, in addition to the base salary, meant not having to travel, not having to meet in person with clients, and not really having to prospect for new clients, as I would only be talking with advisors. It was financial services but business-to-business. This beat the heck out of what I was doing, and already having my licenses meant that I was an attractive candidate.

So I dutifully applied and went through an interview with HR and then was called in for an in-person interview with two managers of internal wholesaling. I was given the typical interview questions and gave the typical BS answers to why I wanted the job. It is a spin that anyone who has failed at one endeavor uses to explain away that failure is all too familiar with. I was looking for "growth" and a "collegial environment," and so forth. Since the two managers had followed the same path I had, they understood that what I really needed was a paycheck!

I then was put through a mock phone call in which I would impersonate an internal wholesaler calling an advisor. All in all, hokey, but I sailed through that and was offered a position. In the end, I imagine that I entered this field like most, with an attitude of gratitude for having a paycheck and utilizing the licenses I had worked hard to obtain and being able to hold myself out to the world as a financial sales professional. The thing that my friends and family probably liked best was that in my capacity as an internal wholesaler, I would not be calling on them!

It would not take long before I realized that this was a heck of a gig. We were paid to talk all day on the phone pitching annuities and mutual funds. We got paid a decent base salary with the opportunity to double that if sales were good. We were not on the hook as sales-people if sales were weak, so there was little stress, and anyway it was 2007, and the market was roaring. My teammates and I used to say that "we had done worse for less." That soon changed to "rarely had we done as little for as much."

Even as 2007 gave way to the market crash years of 2008–2009, the money kept rolling in. Yes, there had been layoffs, but most of us kept our jobs, and even with clients losing billions in asset value, we spun our operation to the fixed interest rate products that were in demand and made an absolute killing compared to the effort we expended. By 2010, the average wholesaler on our team was pulling in six figures. One hundred thousand per year for dialing the phone in Omaha, Nebraska. Are you kidding me! I finally understood why the wholesaler that our field office tried to recruit had scoffed at the notion of going back into personal production. It also, in retrospect, becomes easy to understand why I looked the other way for as long as I did. It becomes easy at that point to rationalize what you do, as conviction so often follows the money.

So what is it that we sold? Garbage for the most part. I mean no product is without some redeeming features, and that was true of the products I wholesaled. One should, in this industry, never say never and never say always. We primarily sold deferred variable annuities, so we tended to see the world through that lens. When you sell ham-mers, everything looks like nails. I don't want to go into excessive detail here. The main point is that these were expensive, high-cost products that, because of the high costs, typically underperformed. However, they paid high commissions for all involved.

The way you sell high-cost, underperforming products is to fill the air with jargon and doublespeak so that you can bamboozle advisors and clients. The profusion of jargon and gobbledygook is intended to befuddle the advisor, who will almost never admit that they do not understand any of this (trust me, most do not). It also serves to give the advisor talking points to befuddle a client who cannot reasonably be expected to understand these concepts or fairly evaluate the competing choices before them. If an advisor can do this, they can get the client to buy almost anything.

So the day-to-day plan was to reach as many advisors as possible and repeat the talking points ad nauseam. In short, baffle them with bunkum until they had learned the story well enough to convince a client. As a famous quote has it, "The secret of success is sincerity. Fake that and you're in."

I need to get a bit more wonkish here to help the reader understand how all this makes money sense. What really makes an advisor commit to selling a fund or annuity and not care about the expense or performance is, not surprisingly, the money—commissions and "marketing support."

Let's mostly skip over commissions. It is enough for our purposes here to say that commissions are high on the products we sold. How else could the pay of a wholesaling team be generated? Of course, commissions always come from the client's account value and every dollar paid out in the form of commissions or expenses reduces the amount of money invested and therefore lowers the client's return. Commissions and client interests are in direct conflict. It might be justifiable if the advisors were giving the clients unbiased advice, but they were not.

The only type of investment advice that could possibly be conflict-free is to charge a client a flat fee to produce a financial plan based on their needs and resources and then have nothing to do with either recommending, selling, or managing the assets. But where's the fun or excessive profit in that?

Neither of the dominant forms of payment arrangements changes the fundamental conflict of interest that exists in this business: that the recommendations themselves are bought and paid for by fund companies and insurance carriers. It is to this topic we turn to next, which is where the true moral compromise comes into play.

There are two ways that advisors are bought: an indirect way and a direct way. Indirectly, advisors are purchased via their back offices.

To fully understand this, I must digress a moment and discuss how the industry is set up. Each advisor affiliates with a broker-dealer. This entity is how an advisor can get his/her clients' money invested in stocks, bonds, mutual funds, and the like. It is the broker/dealers that give advisors access to the markets.

Advisors can be either employees of a broker-dealer (such as bank advisors) or simply contracted with them but employees of an independent firm or self-employed. What is important to understand is that in every transaction, a broker-dealer must act as an intermediary.

Additionally, broker-dealers must perform certain regulatory functions as well as protect themselves from legal liability. Therefore, they provide suitability oversight to determine whether a particular trade is appropriate. This compliance function is important to both the broker-dealers as well as the advisors (which does not mean that clients don't get screwed). Broker-dealers, of course, take a cut of an advisor's commission for these services.

In the competition for advisors, broker-dealers will offer inducements and add-on services. Perhaps they will offer a bonus for a top producer to move their clients from one broker-dealer to another. Also, they all provide value-added services such as business building tools, client management software, and ongoing training and required continuing education.

Even though broker-dealers compete for advisors' business, they have an enormous amount of control over them (especially for those broker-dealers that directly employ advisors). This control extends to choosing which products advisors have available. Every broker-dealer has funds and annuity products that are "preferred." Ostensibly, this means that the back office had carefully analyzed these products and determined that they are the best of the best. That is a quaint idea but hardly one that fits the reality of the situation. The way that funds and annuities become "preferred" is that the broker-dealers are paid to make them so.

They euphemistically call this arrangement revenue sharing. This, in layman's terms, is a kickback or a rebate. For every dollar invested with the above listed fund and annuity companies, those companies kick back a certain percentage. Industry-wide, this adds up to billions of dollars.

The point here is that clients think that they are buying objective advice, but what they are really being sold is deeply compromised advice, which is ill-disclosed.

Equally ill-disclosed are the other ways that fund and annuity companies buy access to advisors through broker-dealer back offices. Chief among these dealings is support for advisor trips and meetings. Advisors, while doing their business, can qualify for award trips and so-called due diligence trips (ostensibly working retreats in a swanky locale). These trips are routinely underwritten to a large degree by one or many fund and annuity companies.

In exchange for these monies to underwrite the trip, the fund and annuity companies get the right to have one of their representatives present to those advisors present. This gives the fund/annuity representatives access to a captive audience of above-average producers to pitch their wares. The quid pro quo occurs when the advisors return to the office and are expected to offer their clients the products they heard presented while on the trip.

Advisors are also bought directly at the street level. Fund and annuity companies give each of their field representatives a budget to use for "marketing support" of advisors. This support can range from basic tchotchkes such as logoed pens, padfolios, stuffed animals to more expensive items such as polo and dress shirts; even watches and other forms of jewelry are available. This process of plying advisors with trinkets is so formalized that all the items available for representatives' use are on a website that resembles a shopping site. The items are ordered, logged against the correct budget account, and sent directly to the advisor if so desired.

In addition to this, there is money provided for support of local advisors' events such as client seminars, client appreciation events, and advisor-client meet and greet events. Rarely, if ever, are the fund and annuity company representatives identified as a partial or full funder of these activities. They are simply identified as experts in the field of investments and retirement planning and serve to add credibility to an advisor's business.

There is even a monetary formula to determining how much money to use in support of an advisor. The rule of thumb in the business is 5 basis points of support for every dollar of production delivered by an advisor. That is 0.0005 percent of sales. If an advisor places a one-million-dollar trade with the company, he/she can expect five hundred dollars of marketing support. I have sat in sales training sessions with these field representatives and seen them specifically trained to proposition an advisor with verbiage such as "I am willing to invest in your business, Mr. Advisor. Are you willing to invest in mine?" When a company spends dollars to have a sales training expert train their sales force on how to extract a quid pro quo from an advisor, something is seriously amiss.

A few anecdotes from my work life should suffice to bring this moral black hole into sharper relief. The following stories are true. I was the wholesaler involved in the interactions with an advisor. I am not using real names of either advisors or their firms to spare them from additional shame over and above being so vile or ignorant.

This set of stories is going to take us deep into the moral sewer. First up is a tale of how broker-dealers view their clients. I, from time to time, was tasked with doing some new advisor training for a broker-dealer that was headquartered in Omaha. This entailed explaining the main features of our basic products and offering a sales idea or two. What the broker dealer mostly wanted was for the new advisors to be given a free dinner, which my employer was happy to do to gain access to new advisors before other carriers and fund companies did.

On the appointed day, I showed up about fifteen minutes early and was directed to the classroom where the training was going on. I sat quietly in the back as the previous training module was wrapping up. On this day, that module was about sales requirements and goal setting. The instructor was going through what was expected of these people as sales reps. She was breaking it down: If you need to hit such and such a revenue goal and the average ticket was so big, then you would have to make X number of sales per week. If, therefore, it took X number of conversations per week to get X number of sales, then you would have to have that number of conversations to hit your goals. In the end, she said you would have to sit across from (here she pointed to a figure on the whiteboard I could not see) this many dollars per day to achieve your sales target. It has always stayed with me that this manager was no longer talking about people, as in actual human beings, but was conceiving of these people as nothing more than dollars. This is tremendously revealing as it underscores how deep the moral rot had gotten in this industry.

This next tale reveals the true mendacity of many advisors. I had an advisor I was working with who was employed by a bank. He was in fact employed by the same bank whose trainer reduced people to mere numbers. He called in to discuss the features of a fixed annuity product that he had recently sold a client. He specifically wanted to know about the commission charge-back features. Commissions are regularly charged back if the contract is surrendered within a year. Different companies have different rules. The company I worked for had strict rules and usually charged back the entire commission if the contract was surrendered within one year.

It is important to understand how this product worked to see just how big a scumbag this advisor was. Almost every annuity has what is called a free withdrawal amount. This is an amount of money that the client can withdraw without incurring a surrender penalty. It is industry standard that this free withdrawal amount is 10 percent of the contract value. If your yearly withdrawal amount is below that 10 percent number, there will be no surrender charge or penalty. Any amount over that free withdrawal amount will be assessed a surrender charge (usually a declining percentage of the contract value as the contract ages).

This product had a client-friendly feature to it that came into play in this situation. If a client completely surrendered the product, they would not be assessed a penalty. It was marketed as a return of premium guarantee. If, however, the client took less than 100 percent of the contract but more than 10 percent, they would be charged a penalty. We would tell advisors to tell their clients to avoid withdrawals between 11 percent and 99 percent of the contract value, or as I would say, "tell your clients to do their walking all at once or not at all."

The problem for advisors is that if a client surrendered all the contract, they would be faced with a commission charge-back. In this situation, the advisor asked what the commission charge-back policy was. I informed him that if the client surrendered the contract, the advisor would have all the commission charged back on the next pay cycle. The advisor then asked if there was a commission charge-back for a 25 percent withdrawal. I knew immediately where this dirt ball was going with his questions. I told him (honestly) that a 25 percent withdrawal by the client would not trigger a commission charge-back but that it would trigger a surrender penalty to the client, a penalty that could be avoided if the client surrendered the entire contract. This made sense, as the product was sold recently enough that if the client needed that much money so quickly, then it was probably not a good idea to have assets tied up in an illiquid product such as an annuity. The advisor probably knew this but did not care, as it would hinder his payday. The advisor quickly brushed past my statements about a course of action that would not adversely affect the client and then said a hurried goodbye to formulate a pitch that would screw the client out of money for no good reason.

This story is only part of a larger pattern regarding early withdrawals and surrender charges. On more than one occasion, I had advisors ask what the ramifications of a large withdrawal would be upon their commissions. This was usually a planned withdrawal within days or weeks of the product being purchased. On one occasion, I had an advisor ask about putting two hundred thousand into an annuity, then what would the consequences be of a fifteen thousand withdrawal. I naively suggested that the advisor just write the sale for 185K and not to have the client penalized or at risk because of the withdrawal. I was ignored, of course. Knowing that all of this was wrong did not stop me from spending years more in this racket.

The next tale reflects another recurring pattern in advisory skullduggery. I had an advisor located in Arizona, prime hunting ground for those without a conscience. This advisor was older himself and openly talked about retiring in a few years. In the meanwhile, I think he figured on having himself a little financial payday before he left the industry. He began to engage in the age-old advisor practice of churning. Churning is simply engaging in excessive trades to generate commissions without benefitting the client. Over the course of six months, this human waste moved most of the clients he had at my company into products at other companies even though each trade resulted in a surrender charge that was paid for by the client. Each step of the way, I gave this prick the verbiage and the intellectual ammunition to "justify" the trades in question. I was giving this guy reasons to move assets away from my company by picking apart the flaws in our products in a way that made them look weaker relative to a competitor's offerings (they were overall about the same). Why would I do this? Because he was bringing us enough new business that there was no reason not to help him in this way. We had already been paid on the contracts he was now moving out, so there was no financial incentive to us directly to try and keep the assets under our management. Our financial incentives were aligned with his—we wanted to get paid, and if that meant helping him justify ways to screw his clients, then we would just turn a blind eye to it.

This story does have a somewhat happy ending. This bozo was so brazened in his actions that even his back office got suspicious and instigated an investigation. I was one of the people they contacted, and I explained truthfully that there appeared to be little justification to the trades he was making, and I gave them honest accounts of what the products did compared to the products he moved them into. The advisor was forced to pay restitution to the clients who had been made to pay surrender penalties, so they were at least made whole. In the end, I did the legally correct thing and told the truth when it absolutely mattered. If I had done the right thing, I would have dropped a dime on this guy and turned him in myself. The human capacity for rationalization is boundless.

This story was repeated in a variety of ways. One of the chief benefits an internal wholesaler can offer an advisor is justification of a trade, any trade. I used to pride myself on my ability to give any advisor the ammunition to win over his back office regardless of the specifics of the case. I would even coach my teammates on such techniques. I called it my "get a pen and paper" spiel.

This scenario occurred more times than I can recount. It usually began with an advisor calling somewhat panicked because the back office was about to reject a trade as unsuitable. Never mind if it was in fact unsuitable, the advisor and the wholesaling team had money on the line! I would calmly inquire as to the specific objection of the back office. Since we mostly sold annuities with an income guarantee feature, the objection typically centered on whether this was appropriate. Let's be clear; sometimes it was a decent solution. There were usually better solutions that paid the client more at lower cost, but there were times when what we were selling produced a good result for the client (not that this concerned us much).

The back office would often object to either the cost of the feature producing the guaranteed income, or they would be concerned with a client tying up too great a percentage of their assets in a relatively illiquid annuity.

In either case, I would tell the advisor to get a pen and paper. I would then launch into the precise verbiage that the advisor would need to convince the back office that this was a good solution for the client. The key is to rearrange the client objectives to match the product being offered. If the client needs guaranteed income in retirement (who doesn't?) then that was to be emphasized. That left the issue of cost. Why would the client choose this option rather than one that yielded as much or more money at lower cost? The answer was that the client may want to have a lump sum available for some emergency or other need that would necessitate a deferred variable annuity with an income benefit rider at a higher cost rather than an immediate annuity where you could not get your money back. Keep in mind this only really mattered if the client was leaving *no* emergency money in their account. Convincing the client to go along with this was easy. They were usually so befuddled by the array of choices and the jargon set before them that scaring them into not wanting to "give up control of their money" was simple.

By giving the advisor the right verbiage to repeat to the back office and getting the client to go along, you could take any situation and turn it inside out and upside down and voila, you have yourself a justifiable sale. The ability to take a malleable client and rearrange the storyline to fit the sales needs of the moment was not really that difficult, but it was and is a critical component of the day-to-day life of a wholesaler.

There is, of course, a whole panoply of minor variations on these stories. As a wholesaler, I helped hundreds of advisors do dicey things to their clients, like ignoring the fact that a rep has a trail of complaints on their record that would shame a con man or perhaps continuing to deal with advisors who only ask what the commission is on your products, never bothering to ask how they work. It was all in a day's work as an internal wholesaler, and if the advisor sold the client, then I got paid as well.

There was even a situation whereby a broker-dealer prohibited the acceptance of freebies and goodies from wholesalers, but this did not stop the advisor from receiving them. My external partner was hosting an event at a major league ballpark in a clubhouse, and pursuant to that, we invited the top reps from one of our top broker-dealer partners. The invites went out via email, and soon after, this advisor emailed back that he would not be attending. *Immediately* after I received that email, the advisor called me directly and said he would, of course, be at the event. The official company policy was to not take such incentives from wholesalers, which is why he wanted his reply on the record in email form. Just another day dodging the compliance officer.

The problem only magnified itself after I took a promotion and became a manager. I was now helping others to screw clients, not just doing it myself. As time went on, I and my colleagues became increasingly and openly jaded. We used to joke that "it is always in the best interests of the client that the advisor gets paid." We had moved beyond actual ignorance, through willful ignorance, to outright cynicism.

I realize this is a deep dive into a subject that is not strictly germane to the overall topic. It is relevant, however, because this is the type of moral compromise many of us face every day in our lives. This is true whether we are faithful or unbelievers. For those of us faithful, who are trying to act as God would have us in response to His gift of salvation, we still need to navigate the moral ambiguities and pitfalls of this world. Your experience will differ in its specifics, depending upon your field of endeavor, but the mechanics of moral compromise are largely the same. No matter if you are a lawyer or in the medical field or selling food or construction equipment, you will face a myriad of opportunities to cut corners, look the other way at ethical compromises, and asked to weigh your family's income in the balance. I took you on a deep dive to illuminate the problem more clearly, even if the specific challenges for the reader are different. If nothing else, you have some insight into how your money management may be compromised.

I do not want to leave the impression that I knew all of this before or even shortly after I went to work in this role. Even *I* was not that cynical. I spent eight years at this company doing this work. By year 4, after the 2007–2008 meltdown, and my promotion, I had enough experience and insight to realize the true nature of this work. Yet I stayed for an additional four years, fully half my time in this field. The money was too much and too easy. It is easy to not listen to God when things are going that well, but there comes a time when you cannot quiet His voice any longer.

I also do not want to leave the impression that everyone in the industry is a jaded, amoral sales robot. Most in the business are simply ignorant of this behind-the-scenes machinations. There are many who are aware of the inherent conflicts and are trying their level best to help their clients avoid the pitfalls. Then there are some brazen crooks who are simply out to make as much money as they can at whatever the cost. Then there are many like the way I used to be, aware of the conflicts but willfully looking the other way.

Moral meltdown: Getting my ears unplugged

The end came when I could no longer live with the cognitive dissonance of a professed set of faith beliefs regarding how one should treat other human beings and the life I was living. In early 2015, I began reading a book, *The Cost of Discipleship*[1] by the acclaimed Lutheran theologian (and martyr to the Nazis) Dietrich Bonhoeffer. This book is an extended commentary on the Sermon on the Mount and what Bonhoeffer thinks it means to be a follower of Jesus. He rolls out a concept of what he calls "cheap grace." He means by this a life lived not really sacrificing anything in response to the grace that Jesus has bestowed upon us. This was a dagger to the entire way I was making money. Combine this damning critique with a birthday and you get a full-blown moral crisis.

So I just quit. I mean I had a near panic attack at the prospect of going to yet another "sales" conference (underwritten by fund companies, of course), and I went into my boss's office and turned in my resignation. I was lucky. I have a spouse who earns enough that I technically didn't have to work, so I had options. There are good people still in that industry who know better yet are trapped. I was blessed by not being one of them.

The point here is that we must continue to listen to God and to understand what He is telling us. This is a noisy world, full of people who offer all sorts of rationales and excuses for doing what we in our hearts know is wrong. We know instinctively what our response to God's gift of salvation should be; we know it deep in our hearts. We know it so well that we are scared witless to acknowledge it openly. The best exposition of this phenomenon comes from the great theologian Soren Kierkegaard:

> The matter is quite simple. The Bible is very easy to understand. But we Christians are a bunch of scheming swindlers. We pretend to be unable to understand it because we know very well that the minute, we understand we are obliged to act accordingly. Take any words in the New Testament and forget everything except pledging yourself to act accordingly. My God, you will say, if I do that my whole life will be ruined. Herein lies the real place of Christian scholarship. Christian

scholarship is the Church's prodigious invention to defend itself against the Bible, to ensure that we can continue to be good Christians without the Bible coming too close. Dreadful it is to fall into the hands of the living God. Yes, it is even dreadful to be alone with the New Testament.[2]

His comments make it abundantly clear why we plug up our ears. However, we can only do that for so long. Eventually, God's message gets through, and since you believe, you must obey. The entire experience was humbling. Far from "having arrived," I needed to continually listen to His message, His good and gracious word. It is the clarity of consistently hearing God's message to us that we have any hope of overcoming our human frailties.

It was from that point on that I finally understood that a relationship with God is an ongoing process, not a one and done arrival point. We only "arrive" when we stand before our Lord when we are all done dancing on this earth. At that point, whether we believe or not is fully known to God, as nothing we do can hide the total truth of who we are. In the meanwhile, we do the best we can and steadily try to seek the good and avoid the bad. The frightening thing is, based on my experience, how long we can delude ourselves into confusing good and bad. Let me be clear; none of what I did put my salvation at risk. If there is not an external work that can merit your salvation, then there is not an external work that can lose that salvation. It was simply a poor response to God's gift and that grates over time. There is, of course, still a thing called sin (and I was sinning here), which I will discuss in the next chapter, yet this is not the same thing as losing your faith, the faith that saves. I also realized that for what I had done, God forgave me. This realization is just a renewed understanding that we are saved by faith.

Forgiveness: That most clarifying of tonics

After leaving the moral quagmire of the financial services field, I began to refocus my faith journey on truly hearing God's word and understanding what He is telling us. This has resulted in a deep dive into the theology of the gospel that was the heart and the best of what Martin Luther taught. But true clarification did not come until forgiveness was both sought and granted.

Forgiveness is core to everything God is communicating to us. It was the core of Jesus's life, death, and resurrection. We are forgiven in baptism; we are forgiven continually by God when we seek it, and we are instructed to forgive one another. As my former pastor put it, "How many times should you forgive? One more time than you think you ought to." In large part, to respond to God's gift of salvation is to live a life of forgiveness, asking and granting.

We understand this in theory and acknowledge it when we recite the Lord's Prayer. However, to live it is another thing altogether. Between forgiving another and asking for forgiveness, the asking strikes me as far more difficult. If we are asked to grant forgiveness, we retain control. We like control. It is why we are so attracted to the damaging theology of works righteousness. It is why we are so stubborn, as Kierkegaard points out, in avoiding submitting all of ourselves to God.

Asking for forgiveness is a great deal more difficult. It is the spiritual equivalent of throwing yourself upon the mercy of the court in a legal proceeding. This is, of course, what we must do in the face of God anyway, but it is terrifying nonetheless. It places us in someone else's control. This is tough enough for us to do before God but intensely difficult to do with another human being.

I found this out firsthand. In August of 2020, I lost an older sister. She was the first of my siblings to die, except for my parents' firstborn, who neither me nor my seven siblings remember. This loss was made more acute by the fact that this older sister was the source of some of my fondest memories growing up, as she was often tasked with taking care of her pain-in-the-ass little brother. In the fullness of time, she came to occupy a special place in my children's lives as well, when she settled into the role of the eccentric aunt. Whether it was baking Christmas cookies or staying with them while my wife and I went out or traveled, neither I nor my children can put into words what she truly meant to us.

During her final days in hospice, I was fortunate to spend some time with her. We had good conversation about our upbringing and fond memories of our parents and childhood experiences. I was able to tell her that I loved her and to say goodbye, with my assurance that I fully planned on seeing her on the other side.

All of this may sound poignant, but it is more so because it almost did not happen. You see, between about 2014 and the year prior to her death, I had no real relationship with her. The relationship was broken, and I was the one who broke it. I am not going into the details of this except to say it was part of some broader large family dysfunction. I could claim that I was the youngest and was just going along with the big group, but when you are a grown-ass man in his fifties, you must own what you do in this world.

I was fortunate to have God speaking to me through my wife and my therapist (more on her in just a bit). I became convicted of the reality that I was a part of a wrongful and hurtful treatment of my sister, and that literally *by* God, I had to attempt to make it right. So I penned an email. I knew she would not take a meeting with me nor open a letter, but I figured an email might catch her attention just long enough for me to get her to read what I wanted to tell her. Here is a part of what I wrote:

> I am writing this letter to apologize and ask your forgiveness for my part in the way you were treated. To my great shame I did not push back on that idea hard enough nor did I communicate to you that it was not the way I truly felt about the situation. I have no excuse for why I acquiesced in this, but it is likely explained by the fact that I felt guilty over not carrying my fair share of the load in Mom and Dad's care, a load that disproportionately fell upon you. Regardless, I can do nothing now but to ask your forgiveness.
>
> It is with these things in mind that I was prompted to write this letter. I am simply not willing to

let this relationship go without reaching out to apologize for the damage I have done to it, it is a relationship that, quite simply means too much to me. It is necessary for me that you know how sorry I am and that regardless of your response to this letter I love you and will always do so to the end.

I have never written more difficult nor more important words in my life. I was scared senseless when I sent the email. I guessed that I would get no response, and I was not about to blame her for that. To my shock, but not my therapist's, she did respond. It was a cautious response but a hopeful one. In short order, it turned into a reconciliation between us. The relationship was never quite what it was before, but there was a relationship, and it was good. It is one of the most grace-filled acts I have ever had directed at me.

What I learned most deeply is that it is important to go about seeking forgiveness sooner rather than later. If you have a relationship that needs repair, do not wait until it is too late to try to fix it, because one day it will be. There are no do-overs. It terrifies me to think that my sister would have died without my having made the choice to apologize. Going forward in life with that on your conscience is not something that I would wish upon anyone.

None of this is easy, nothing of value ever is. In making the attempt to right what you made wrong, you put yourself on the right side of God and the right side of your humanity. Also, while you may not get the response you hope for, you might just get a Christ-filled act of grace that will fill your heart forevermore. To this day I remain humbled by her response and grateful beyond measure that I understood God most clearly in that moment.

As I stated, asking forgiveness is, I think, much more difficult than granting it. This is not to say that granting forgiveness is easy. Hurt and betrayal cut deep and are not easily shaken off. My pastor once said that he did not think it was a sin to not forgive someone, but that it was a sin to not *want* to. We are human; we will not always succeed in doing what we should or what we desire. The best advice

I can give is to focus on God's forgiveness of us as a springboard for forgiving others. In the face of what God has given us and forgiven us for, it seems trite in comparison to let go of the wrongs others have committed against us.

There is one type of forgiveness, though, that is excruciatingly difficult to grant, or should I say, one person who is most difficult to forgive: yourself. My forgiveness of myself came through the therapeutic process.

I am not going to burden you with a lot of details. Suffice it to say that I suffered from panic attacks and a high degree of anxiety. It got to the point that it was interfering with routine aspects of my life. So out of more desperation than anything else, I sought help. I was incredibly fortunate to find a gifted counselor who quickly (scarily quick) got to the root of what was ailing me.

What was ailing me was that I had not forgiven myself for the egregious things I had done in my past, particularly those that surrounded my drunkenness. For over thirty years, I carried buried within myself the pain and the shame of what I had done as a drunken fool. I was able by way of this process to first give voice to what I had done. For the first time, I spoke aloud my rock-bottom experience of not being able to recognize my own father's voice that drunken night on the telephone. I spoke openly about the pain of having, on multiple occasions, almost killed people I love very much because I was moronic enough to get behind the wheel of a car while completely smashed.

The guilt I carried was crushing and getting worse, not better. Time may heal old wounds but not before you drain the infection and treat the wound. In giving voice to this pain, shame, and guilt, I was able to remove much of the power my past had over me. I was finally able to forgive the young, drunken fool who committed these wrongs. I came to realize that God had long since forgiven me of all of this and much more. It was long past time that I caught up with God and forgave myself.

In finally forgiving myself, combined with my experience in asking and being granted forgiveness, I heard the gospel more clearly than I have ever before in my life. God speaks to us and works on this earth through the people in our lives. This is true whether they realize it or not. The message that I finally heard with utmost clarity is that God loves us more than we could possibly love Him. God wants a relationship with us more than we could possibly want a relationship with Him. He loves us so much that He sent His Son to live among us as one of us. Everything we experience God experienced through Jesus. God's full, complete love and forgiveness *is* the good and gracious word; this is the good news. Because God had said it, we simply believe. Nothing could be clearer than that. The thing that remains to examine is, now that I understand much more clearly, what do *I* propose to do with this good news?

10

Toward a Re-reformation

What is the question?

This is the chapter that contains the most formal theology. I make no apologies for this. These are concepts that are accessible to lay people without formal theological training. I know that for many this is eyes-glaze-over stuff, yet these concepts are crucial to understanding what God is telling us. All the damaging consequences that I experienced because of a theology of works righteousness and the state of unbelief I ended in could have been avoided if a proper understanding of what God was saying was communicated. History and our current age are full of deleterious consequences from an erroneous understanding of God. Just because that is the historical reality is no reason to think that it must continue. It did not continue for me once I made it out of the wilderness into the clearing of belief and forgiveness. I now have tremendous clarity, and that clarity can be established by grappling with some accessible theological concepts that make God understandable to us. On to it.

The question is simple: what if anything is wrong with works? First, it is an important question. We seek the truth in God's word, and all the faithful are sincerely striving to clearly understand what God is telling us. If we are wrong, we want to know it. If *I* am wrong, I want someone to show me so. Second, it is appropriate and fairer to frame the question this way, as a negative. The reason is simple;

everybody believes that you need faith to be justified before God. The Catholic formulation is faith and works, so it's right there in the first word. Of course, Catholics believe in faith as well as grace as a gift from God. However, Catholics, and many Protestants, as we shall see, think that works are also needed. Therefore, the negative framing of this question is the best framing. Before that we must establish that works is indeed still a thing.

Are works really still a thing?

Sadly, the answer is yes, works righteousness is still very much a thing. The most prominent purveyor of this theology is, of course, the Roman Catholic Church. It is and always has been a formal part of their dogma since at least the time of Augustine, who lived from about AD 354–430.

Augustine was certainly a believer in grace as a gift from God. He felt that even our love for God was a gift from God. According to Augustine, we ourselves cannot come to love God, so without the gift of grace, we would die in our sins. However, Augustine also held that as we grow in love and obedience to God, we can become better and more worthy through our own efforts. Granted, you received the ability to do meritorious works from God, but you by your free will could do them. Augustine would hold then that we can strengthen our justification before God by our meritorious works. It might be analogized as becoming stronger by walking via our efforts on a long road, as opposed to Martin Luther, who described it as receiving a gift from God. Therefore, faith *and* works have been a part of the Catholic tradition from its earliest days. Keep in mind that just because Augustine thought this does not make it so.

Works remained a part of the Catholic tradition in the aftermath of the Reformation. It is important to note that the entire Reformation controversy began with the sale of indulgences and Martin Luther's rejection of them as inconsistent with the gospel.

Indulgences are a means by which the faithful may reduce the punishment one has to undergo for sins committed. As the Catholic Catechism states, an indulgence is "a remission before God of the temporal punishment due to sins whose guilt has already been forgiven, which the faithful Christian who is duly disposed gains under certain prescribed conditions through the action of the Church which, as the minister of redemption, dispenses and applies with authority the treasury of the satisfactions of Christ and all of the saints."[1] The "certain prescribed conditions" was usually the payment of monies. This was in fact how the pope was raising money for the building of St. Peter's Basilica.

This is important to note because indulgences are absolutely not possible without an underlying theology of the necessity of works. If Luther's theology had been dominant, no one would have ever considered payment of monies for the forgiveness of sins. Everyone would have especially rejected the notion of payment of monies to get dead family out of purgatory sooner.

The official theological response by the Catholic Church to the Reformation was the Council of Trent, which ran from 1545–1563. The official response of this council could not have been clearer; Catholic dogma would embrace faith and works. Again, I am not stating that Catholics do not believe in faith or God's gift of mercy; of course, they do. I am simply stating what they themselves admit, that works are a part of obtaining salvation.

In the official documents of the Council of Trent, the church stated, concerning Justification:

> Having, therefore, been thus justified [by God's Grace originally], and made the friends and domestics of God, advancing from virtue to virtue, they are renewed, as the Apostle says, day by day; that is, by mortifying the members of their own flesh, and by presenting them as instruments of justice unto sanctification, they, through the observance of the commandments of God and of the Church, faith co-operating with good works, increase in that justice which they have received through the grace of Christ, and are still further justified, as it is written; He that is just, let him

be justified still; and again, Be not afraid to be justified even to death; and also, Do you see that by works a man is justified, and not by faith only. And this increase of justification holy Church begs, when she prays, Give unto us, O Lord, increase of faith, hope, and charity.[2]

These decrees from the Council of Trent are currently considered infallible. They are notably not considered the highest level of infallibility, the so-called *de fide credenda*, which means part of the deposit of faith. These decrees are considered *de fide tenenda* or contingent on historical facts, due to the historical controversy surrounding the Reformation. This means they may move to the higher level of infallibility or perhaps go the other way. I will discuss more about this a bit later. Nonetheless, the decrees of the Council of Trent are currently binding upon the Catholic conscience.

The other place that the church clearly endorses the theology of works is in its current catechism. Section 2010 lays it out clearly:

Since the initiative belongs to God in the order of grace, no one can merit the initial grace of forgiveness and justification, at the beginning of conversion. Moved by the Holy Spirit and by charity, we can then merit for ourselves and for others the graces needed for our sanctification, for the increase of grace and charity, and for the attainment of eternal life. Even temporal goods like health and friendship can be merited in accordance with God's wisdom. These graces and goods are the object of Christian prayer. Prayer attends to the grace we need for meritorious actions.[3]

None of this is hidden or in any way a conspiracy. All of this is out in the open. You can find the complete Catholic Catechism online or get a copy in a bookstore. They are not trying to hide any of this. It remains a theology that is taught and prescribed. There is still quite extant in the Catholic tradition the need to do external works and meritorious actions to secure your salvation. It is downplayed among many, I think, because of a variety of factors, some of which I will discuss, but it *is* still a formal part of Catholic dogma.

Certainly, works are not a Protestant thing, right?

Sadly, works righteousness is indeed a Protestant thing. In fact, I would argue that it is a more insidious thing among the Protestant faith communities than the Catholic Church. Catholics are, as we have seen, quite open about their belief in the need for works as a part of justification. Protestants, on the other hand, deny any such beliefs. It is like trying to get a drunk to stop drinking via a 12-step program, but they will not get past step one, admitting that they have a problem. Well, Protestants *have* a problem.

Formally, Protestants do reject the notion of necessary works. This flows from Martin Luther's insights regarding salvation through faith alone at the start of the Reformation. Protestants hold that grace is just a name for God being gracious toward us, not a thing that is created in us. Therefore, grace is not formed or enhanced by habits or something we can possess in our souls. Also, Protestants hold that grace is not the basis of merit the way Catholics believe. Nor can grace be acquired by practice, even practicing the sacraments, that would make it a work.

Much Protestant theology claims, therefore, that our souls are not inwardly formed by grace. Justification would therefore not make any real change in us but simply means having one's sins forgiven. The Holy Spirit does work a change in us, but this comes *afterward* and is what impels us to serve others *because* of the receipt of this gift.

In all of this, I am indebted to Phillip Cary, professor of philosophy at Eastern University in St. Davids, Pennsylvania. Allow me to quote from his course guidebook *Luther: Gospel, Law, and Reformation:*

> This means that the righteousness we receive when we are justified by faith alone is not a form,

habit, or virtue in our souls but, rather, the righteousness of Christ imputed to us, a verdict of "innocent" pronounced over us when the merits of Christ are transferred, as it were, to our account.

The doctrine that the righteousness received by faith is not a real change in us but only a verdict and imputation of innocence is called the *forensic* doctrine of justification (from the Latin word *forum*, meaning "courtroom").

Luther's doctrine of justification, it can be argued, is not primarily forensic: The righteousness of God is not merely imputed to us but is the righteousness of Christ dwelling in us.

What forms our hearts, according to Luther, is Christ, received by hearing the Word. Luther is willing to use the language of a "form" in the soul, so long as it is understood that this form is not a habit or virtue or created grace but Christ himself, dwelling in the heart by faith.

There are two ways our souls can be formed, according to Aristotle: not only by practice but also by perception, as an eye is informed by what it sees. Luther is willing to accept the second way of forming our inmost souls not by practice (good works) but by perception (hearing the Gospel and believing it). Through faith in the Gospel, Christ himself dwells in us and is our righteousness, and this re-forms our souls from the bottom up. Luther's view is, thus, both a critique of the Catholic theology of grace and an attempt to achieve some of its goals by means of a different set of concepts.

A non-forensic reading of Luther's doctrine of justification runs contrary to the mainstream of Lutheran theology but has much in its favor.

Luther does speak of imputation, but it is not at the heart of his doctrine of justification. For Luther, it can be argued, the righteousness of God is in us through faith in Christ (that's central), but sin also remains in us (because we are *simul justus et peccator*, righteous and sinner at the same time); therefore, for Christ's sake, God does not impute our sins to us.

Such a reading of Luther avoids the common Protestant trap of making Christ a means rather than an end, as if he were only a technique for acquiring the status of righteousness, rather than God in person.[4]

You should be able to immediately see the trap that Professor Cary mentions. If we make Christ a means to "impute" grace unto ourselves, add more credits than debits to our account, so to speak, then it becomes about what we are doing, not what God is doing. It becomes a work that we perform, not a gift we receive. It turns the proper relationship with God on its head. We forget the fundamental reality of this universe: God is God, and we are not.

The genesis of the theology of works is the desire for humanity to be in control. This is what lead to the fall, in the creation story in the book of Genesis. The serpent promised that if Adam and Eve ate the fruit from the tree of forbidden knowledge, "for God knows that when you eat of it your eyes will be opened, and you will be like God, knowing good and evil." (Genesis 3:5). Humanity has been stumbling over this problem ever since. Protestants are certainly not immune from the seductiveness of this perspective.

Much of Protestant theology veered off into the wrongheaded understanding of Luther's insights. Most of the main branches of Protestantism reflect this "forensic" view of justification. This even includes much of the Lutheran community. Subtly, over time, the view came to dominate that we had to credit our account with righteousness by means of Christ rather than accepting Christ as an end unto Himself. From there it was only a matter of time before a list of things to be done was drawn up, and we had to engage in external actions or works to get more credits than debits added to our account.

This is not an idea I arrived at but forms the core of a seminal book by a respected Lutheran theologian, Gerhard Forde. In his 1972 *Where God Meets Man* effort, Forde outlines what he terms "ladder theology." This is as it sounds an attempt by humans to climb a ladder to God. It is the outgrowth of a distorted view of man's relationship to God and the misinterpreting of Luther's theological insights.

As Forde states:

> What is wrong with our usual understanding of the Christian faith[?] We tend to think it has to do primarily with "going up" somewhere—either to heaven or to some kind of "religious perfection." The Christian faith is often likened to climbing a ladder or, if you will, a staircase. Take, for example, the symbol of "Jacob's ladder." In the middle ages it was popular, especially among mystics, as a symbol of the struggle the Christian must undertake to reach perfection...
>
> **The difficulty with the idea of the ladder, however, is that it tends to send us off into the wrong direction. It tends to make us concerned with works of pious sublimation; it involves us in the task of ascending to heaven when we should be seeking like our Lord to come down to earth, to learn what it means to be a Christian here on this earth...**
>
> The troublesome question of the nature of law and gospel and the relationship between them... it is here, in the question of the law and the gospel, that our incurable tendency to go "up the down staircase" is most apparent... **The main trouble is that this "ladder theology" inevita-**

133

bly distorts our understanding of the gospel. The gospel is taken captive by the system and turned into a new kind of law... The gospel comes to make up for the deficiencies of the law. The gospel does not come as anything really new. It is not the breaking in of a radically new age with an entirely new outlook. It is simply "a repair job." ...The net result is that the gospel itself simply becomes another kind of law.[5]

As the title of the book implies, we do not have to climb a ladder to God. God has come down to earth to be among us and to be one of us. All we need do is to receive this gift, to simply believe. The opposite of this simple belief is what Forde terms "An Absurd Theology," the notion that anyone, even Jesus, can buy off God or that we can be certain that Jesus has paid enough or that if God is paid off, how can we say we have been forgiven?[6]

Forde steers us to Luther's key insight that the "law" serves to alert us to the conviction that we as sinners need help. That help is the gospel. Upon hearing God's good and gracious word, we simply believe and are so saved. We are changed and the righteousness of Christ dwells within us.

The initial misinterpretation of Luther led to an inevitable focus of what we should *do* rather than what God is doing. This led to changing the Gospel into another statement of law, which led people to preach a list of things we need to do or rungs on a ladder to ascend to reach God. The truly damaging thing about all this works righteousness in the Protestant world is that it is shrouded by incessant claims that we are saved by faith alone. The in-the-street reality is that few really think that this is so and is the source of much damage to the faithful and those who might be drawn to the cross. Sadly, it only got worse as time went on.

It is so bad today that in a study published in 2017 by the Pew Research Center, 52 percent of *Protestants* believed that good deeds are needed for salvation.[7] In the United Kingdom and Germany

(Home of the Reformation!), the number holding that works are necessary is over 60 percent.[8]

The Genesis of Protestant works righteousness

The move to a forensic view of imputed righteousness began as early as the Augsburg Confession of 1530. Luther was still alive, but this part was written by his trusted friend Philipp Melanchthon. This is taken from the Augsburg Confession Article IV:

> Men cannot be justified before God by their own strength, merits, or works, but are *freely justified for Christ's sake, through faith, when they believe that they are received into favor*, and that their sins are forgiven for Christ's sake, who, by His death, has made satisfaction for our sins. This faith God *imputes for righteousness in His sight*.[9]

This is not a clear break but is a step away from the best interpretation of Luther's thoughts on justification.

Later in the sixteenth century, the Reformed Tradition, which came out of Switzerland with Huldrych Zwingli and is most famously represented by John Calvin, moved more clearly in the direction of having righteousness imputed and our accounts credited. In the Heidelberg Catechism published in 1563, the language has shifted:

Q & A 61
Q. Why do you say that through faith alone you are righteous?
A. Not because I please God by the worthiness of my faith.
It is because only Christ's satisfaction, righteousness, and holiness make me righteous before God, and because I can accept this righteousness

and make it mine in no other way than through faith.

Q & A 62

Q. Why can't our good works be our righteousness before God, or at least a part of our righteousness?

A. Because the righteousness which can pass God's judgment must be entirely perfect and must in every way measure up to the divine law. But even our best works in this life are imperfect and stained with sin.[10]

The word *imputation* does not appear but seems strongly implied. As the religious author Amy Mantravadi points out: "Notice the shift from the language of *faith* being imputed to 'satisfaction, righteousness, and holiness' being imputed *by* faith."[11] Clearly, Christ has become a means and not an end.

This notion was further codified in the Second Helvetic Confession (A reformed Church gathering) in 1566 (Chapter XV), which stated:

> For Christ took upon himself and bore the sins of the world and satisfied divine justice. Therefore, solely on account of Christ's sufferings and resurrection God is propitious with respect to our sins and does not impute them to us, but *imputes Christ's righteousness to us as our own* (II Cor. 5:19 ff.; Rom. 4:25), so that now we are not only cleansed and purged from sins or are holy, but also, *granted the righteousness of Christ*, and so absolved from sin, death and condemnation, are at last righteous and heirs of eternal life. Properly speaking, therefore, God alone justifies us, and justifies only on account of Christ, *not imputing sins to us but imputing his righteousness to us*.[12]

The danger is clear; if Christ is a means and He is imputing God's righteousness to us, then the question arises: What shall we *do* to get Christ to impute this righteousness to us? A means is a thing *we* can manipulate and control. Think of a pen on your desk; if it is a means and not an end, I manipulate it to write a note, which is the end desired. If the pen is an end unto itself and not merely a means, then it is a thing I grasp. In this way, an end unto itself is a thing we seek and, in the case of Christ, a promise we simply *believe.*

The other serious theological problem with conceiving of Christ as a means to attain the righteousness of God is that to do so separates God and Christ. The notion of a three-in-one triune God stands at the heart of the Christian faith: Catholic and Protestant. It is the central mystery of the Christian faith but crucial to our understanding. It is a part of *every* creedal confession that is embraced by those who call themselves Christian.

To in any way separate the Son from the Father stands in opposition to that creedal confession. The Nicene Creed states it very clearly that Jesus is "God from God, Light from Light, true God from true God; begotten not made, one in being with the Father." It strikes me as illogical that Christ can be a means to God's righteousness unless He is not "one in being with the Father." One in being means that Jesus is God, and therefore, He is the righteousness of God Himself. It may seem a subtle shift, but it is a crucial one.

This shift was exacerbated by the Calvinist insistence that one could tell whether a person was saved by their actions, which demonstrated their faith. This is a slippery slope, as one acts righteous to prove to the community that they are saved (and not be shunned or banned). The works become the thing to demonstrate your faith, and by implication, to get saved, not a thing you do because God gave you this awesome gift.

The fork in the road, then, is the distinction between the "forensic" and non-forensic views of how we are justified before God. Take the forensic fork and eventually you end up in some form of works righteousness. Keep to the non-forensic road and there is a much better chance of avoiding this trap, although we must always be on guard.

The slide into Protestant works righteousness

As I indicated at the beginning of this work, there is more nuance to both the Catholic and Protestant views on justification and how works fit into it than I can go into in an effort such as this. There are and have always been sincere theological efforts to parse this nuance and better understand God's word.

These sincere efforts go all the way back to the scholars who deeply studied the Torah and made its meaning clear. These efforts were certainly part of the early church fathers' attempt to understand the meaning of the New Covenant of Jesus Christ. This includes such monumental efforts as those of Augustine and many who followed him. This sincerity extends through the Reformers and all the way to our day. These efforts did deal with much of the nuance that is inherent in such an effort. I have focused on the single most important nuance that I sincerely believe makes the most difference in our clear understanding of God's message to humanity.

For all this sincerity, the reality at street level is always very different. Messages get garbled and frankly bastardized to mean what the "man on the street" wants it to mean. People in their day-to-day lives do not do nuance very well. We tend to like easy to digest slogans.

This devolution of complex and nuanced ideas invariably tends to self-righteousness. We want control, and what better control can we have than to be able to make ourselves righteous. Humans have, it seems, an endless ability to turn anything into a theology of works. Sadly, this applies to many of our Reformed brothers and sisters.

This slide into self-righteousness took root before Jesus began His ministry. The Pharisees, whom Jesus criticized harshly, were an outstanding example of what happens at the street level. They took the Torah and turned it into a cult of picayune, petty rules and regulations. These were designed to maximize the control of the Pharisees as a class of people and serve to put humanity firmly in control and not God, no matter their protestations to the contrary.

This street-level phenomenon was true in Luther's time as the Catholic Church had become deeply corrupted by the earthly wealth and power that a doctrine of self-righteous works gave them over the faithful. This, to Martin Luther's horror, saw Johann Tetzel quite effectively selling indulgences (get out of purgatory passes for dead relatives) so that the pope could fill his coffers and build a monument to excess known as St. Peter's Basilica—works on steroids.

This continues into our time. What authority do you think a goofy Jesuit is drawing from when he claims that salvation is akin to earning a varsity letter? The authority of works, that's what.

If we as humans are the one's manipulating the means of our salvation and are in some fashion in control of it, the street-level response will be to use this as a tool of control and exclusion and a means to exercise power over others. This is true if that source of self-righteousness comes from an outright claim to such authority, as in Catholic dogma or as an outgrowth of a flawed theology as in the Protestant tradition. It always ends up at the same spiritual dead end.

This is true mainly because we cannot help ourselves. I mean, we are essentially awful creatures. Humanity is notable by our awfulness. Human history is a monument of this reality. The truly good news is that God knows this about us and loves us anyway. This is also, I think, why God has communicated to us that we simply need to trust His good and gracious word and believe in Him. Our essential awfulness means that we cannot for a moment deviate from the radical nature of the gospel, that it is all in God's hands, and that God and God alone is responsible for our salvation. To simply believe is enough, and to go further is to start down the road that leads inevitably to a series of monumentally awful works.

Historical examples of Protestant works righteousness

This chart gives some indication of the various denominations and faith traditions that came from Matin Luther's initial stand against the church in Rome. You can see right away the complexity of this history.

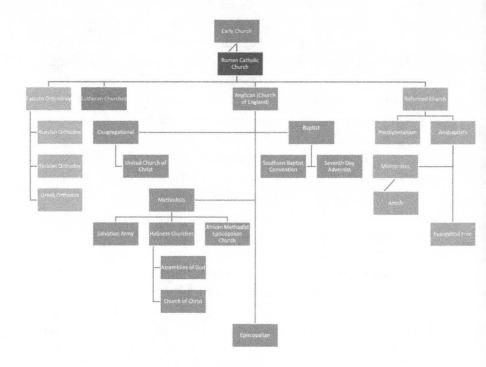

Except for a small group in the Lutheran tradition, almost *every* other branch that grew from the Reformation took the "forensic" fork in the road. This should provide some insight as to the magnitude of the problem.

In time, most Protestant denominations took the lead in rolling out a program of works. All the while denying it was works, of course. This effort started before the end of the sixteenth century. I will outline a few of the more notable examples to establish the point. The first notable example is that of the Calvinists.

John Calvin, following the work of Huldrych Zwingli, came to be one of the major forces in Reformation theology. Soon his views came to dominate theological thinking. Formally called Reformed theology, it often was referred to as Calvinism. It is the Reformed tradition that gave us this forensic view of imputed righteousness. It was the Reformed movement that took the first steps down that fork in the road.

It was the Calvinists who gave rise to what Max Weber in the early twentieth century called the Protestant work ethic. It was this culture he claimed that gave rise to the capitalist ethos of the western world. It is a largely ignored thesis today, especially given the historical work identifying Catholic northern Italy as the cradle of capitalism. Yet it was notable that after several hundred years, the culture generated by Reform theology was so closely tied to this culture of work. Given what Calvin and his followers taught, it was not unreasonable to link his theology to this culture even if capitalism rose in other areas for other reasons.

As indicated, it was the Reformed tradition that gave us the forensic view of salvation. Also, part of Calvin's theology was that once you gained your salvation, you could not lose it. So if you later renounced God or were found to be lacking faith, that just meant that you never had it to begin with.

For Calvin, the main way to determine if someone had faith was to view their actions. Sanctification would be living in response to your salvation. If they lived a righteous life, that would be proof that they were saved, that they were a member of the "elect." Formally, of course, it was salvation "by faith alone," but you would know someone was saved by their works.

As always occurs the notion of sanctification and establishing "proof" of your salvation devolved into prescribed works. Knowing if someone is saved by their outward works devolves into the necessity of performing the works themselves. In the case of the Reformed tradition, this meant working hard—nose to the grindstone, shoulder to the wheel stuff. Frugality was surely a sign, as was being sober-minded, and just plain sober for that matter. Your outward prosperity, or at least your economic self-sufficiency, became the outward sign of righteousness. This loomed especially important as the idea embodied within Reformed theology was that the "elect" was a limited number. It certainly did not hurt that being such a sober, frugal, civic-minded person was good for business and one's place in the community. One can see the faint outlines of a late-twentieth-century phenomenon that I will discuss shortly, that of the notion of the prosperity gospel, which turns on the idea that if you do the right things (like sending money), you will receive nice things in return. I would label all this as right-wing works righteousness. Much of this can be found in *The Idea of Work in Europe from Antiquity to Modern Times.*[13]

All of this not surprisingly culminated in theocracy. By the 1550s, John Calvin had managed to set up in Geneva a theocratic government. This created a monopoly on public preaching by those so "authorized." Worship attendance was, of course, forced as was the observance of the Sabbath. There was also enumerated a series of daily disciplines for the faithful to observe. I will restate this again, but there is no greater proof of a regime of works righteousness than the erection of a theocracy to impose these external works on the population. This was certainly true of the next group to consider, the Puritans.

The Puritans were not a monolithic group, to say the least. They were a multifaceted movement whose main commonality was a desire to get back to the pure basics of the Christian faith. They themselves did not use the term *puritan*; it was thrust upon them by those who opposed them, and the term was largely out of use by the eighteenth century. The main group of Puritans were a minority sect within the Church of England who desired to remove any remaining vestiges of the Roman Catholic tradition.

As for their beliefs, they explicitly followed the Calvinist notion of a forensic imputation of God's grace via Christ. In other words, they rejected the idea of Jesus *as* the righteousness of God.

They also did adhere to the so-called 39 Articles of the Church of England, which in its early form explicitly endorsed the necessity of doing "good works."[14] In its final form, it did reject the notion formally, but it did water down some of the more radical Lutheran influences regarding this doctrine.

The Puritans greatly desired to remove all Catholic influences from the Church of England. This meant affirming only two sacraments (baptism and communion), in similar fashion to the Lutherans. Also, they wanted an end to Episcopal church governance, which involves bishops and so forth, in a manner like the Catholic tradition. They desired a Presbyterian governance, which meant the center of church leadership would be at the congregational level.

As for conversion, they maintained the need for a specific process that *must* take place. There were distinct phases: Bible study, listening to preaching, followed by humiliation (the acknowledgment of their sinful nature), then the imputation of God's grace. There followed a prolonged period of introspection to verify that conversion had in fact occurred. This would be followed by sanctification (which involves behavior). All of this strikes one as itself a series of works that must be performed to be considered converted. As the historian Perry Miller claimed, the Puritans "liberated men from the treadmill of indulgences and penances but cast them on the iron couch of introspection."[15],[16]

Given this focus on introspection and the keeping of detailed records of behaviors after a purported conversion, it is not difficult to see what would happen at the street level when this process was applied. Its application was nothing short of theocracy. The Puritans, who in a short time left for America, as they were not satisfied with the reforms to the Church of England, had set up a rigorous regime of dos and don'ts for the faithful. This included a strong emphasis on family life, a prohibition of gambling and drinking, the outlawing of Christmas and Easter celebrations, and the legal enforcement of the Sabbath. Penalties could include beatings, imprisonment, or outright banishment. There is nothing that screams works righteousness than the use of the power of the government to enforce your ideas of the Christian good. This would continue with the next group I would like to cover, the left wing of the works righteousness brigade, those advancing the social gospel.

The social gospel stems from a rise in pietism. Pietism is the view that we must live a righteous life full of good actions. The idea is that we are called to live a pious life. The idea that we should focus on piety began to stir in the early to middle of the nineteenth century in the United States. Most of the creedal denominations (those that focused on the traditional creeds and communal worship and dogma), the Catholics, Lutherans, and Anglicans, had by this time backed away from serious notions of theocracy. This was especially the case after the secularizing influences of the American and French revolutions.

In the aftermath of these secularizing influences, a pushback occurred as part of the Great Awakening. This became a fervent movement that saw an explosion of religiosity and pietism. This era saw the rise of the Church of Jesus Christ Latter Day Saints (the Mormons), as well as the end-time Millerite movement that morphed into the Seventh Day Adventists.

Broadly, there rose two types of pietism, roughly geographic in nature. There was the southern individualistic piety. This focused on one's individual relationship to Jesus and a personal conversion experience. This personal experience was to be intensely emotional, almost mystical. In this one would be "born again." It is the moment of personal conversion that becomes most important for this mindset. We see here the beginnings of the notion of "decision theology" that today calls for people to "decide for Christ." I will comment on them a bit later.

In contrast, the north of the United States saw the rise of what is best termed an evangelical pietism. This stressed the need to spread holiness and the need to live a pious, holy life. Part and parcel to this mindset was the idea that it was *necessary* to one's salvation to try and ensure all of society's salvation. To this end, these evangelical pietists wanted to stamp out sin. They drew up a list of the usual suspects— drinking, gambling, not honoring the Sabbath, and so forth.

As the nineteenth century moved along, this morphed into what today we recognize as the social gospel. This movement was not monolithic, to say the least, but there were common threads running through most everybody who embraced this approach. First, they were believers in postmillennialism. This is the doctrine that first, we set up the kingdom of God on earth, for one thousand years, then Jesus returns. This is opposed to premillennialism, which holds that first, Jesus returns, *then* He builds His one thousand-year Kingdom. Both views are opposed to amillennialism, which holds that nobody knows when and/or how Jesus will return. This is the view of the creedal denominations.

It should be clear where postmillennialism takes you. If it is necessary to build the kingdom of God on earth before Jesus will return, then you better get busy doing just that. This view was not at all hesitant to endorse concerted societal action via the government to do what needed to be done. This merged nicely with the growing collectivist thought that was emerging mid-nineteenth century. The proponents of the social gospel openly sought state power to bring salvation to society.

The leading lights in this movement were all religious men: Washington Gladden (1836–1918) and Walter Rauschenbusch (1861–1918) were both clergymen. Rauschenbusch wrote his definitive work in 1917 called *A Theology for the Social Gospel*.[17] In it he advocated for an institutional response to sinfulness via the state.

Their agenda was rather all-encompassing. They desired pietist control of education, especially to defeat the growth of the influx of Catholic immigrants. They worked for prolabor legislation and industrial democracy, as well as anti-monopoly legislation. They wanted increased governmental regulation of the economy, especially at the federal level. This helped fuel the creation of agencies such as the Food and Drug Administration and the Federal Reserve. They also wanted and got an aggressive United States foreign policy to help further along global salvation. This reached its apogee in President Wilson's call to make the "world safe for democracy."[18]

There was also a cultural and social dimension to all of this. They worked for an expansion of suffrage to women and, of course, the prohibition of alcohol. This culminated in the passage of much legislation in what came to be known as the Progressive Era, the final piece of which was the Eighteenth Amendment to the US constitution, which outlawed alcohol. Their work continued well into the twentieth and twenty-first centuries in the form of the New Deal and the Great Society and can be seen today in the call for even more concerted action to address racial and gender inequities even if the openly religious only represent a small fraction of this movement today.

This is more accurately defined as a left-wing works righteousness, as opposed to the right-wing version discussed above. What cannot be gainsaid is that it is indeed a dogma of works righteous-ness, as these external actions or works become necessary for salva-tion of both individual and society. Their insistence on concerted state action is also consistent with the Calvinists and the Puritans; it can only be considered theocratic, with all the works righteousness implications involved.

The Puritans have faded from view, at least formally, although their spirit continues in many various ways. Traces of their ideas can be seen in the Moral Majority type fundamentalism that rose in the 1970s. These groups were mostly premillennial in outlook but had become willing to use the state to manipulate Jesus into coming back to inaugurate His one thousand-year reign. They also, like the social gospel folks, wanted concerted state action on a list of causes and policies they wanted enacted. The Calvinists and the social gospel movements are also certainly still extant. They and their theology are spread out amongst the Protestant faithful, so much so that much of what they erected in the way of works righteousness is simply assumed; you are obligated at some level to do good works as a part of attaining your salvation.

In addition to these movements, there are two more modern iterations of the works mentality that I wish to briefly discuss. First is what is called decision theology. This is the notion that one must make a conscious decision in favor of Christ. You must "accept" Him into your life and experience a singular "born again" moment. This is a theology that is prevalent in the Baptist and Methodist traditions but seems to be most widespread amongst the nondenominational fundamentalist congregations. There is a fair amount of overlap between these groups and the remnants of Puritan theology.

The obvious problem with this decision theology is that the onus of salvation is put entirely on humans. We are totally in con-trol as to our salvation. We decide or not; we accept or not. This is as much an external work as anything I have outlined regarding the other historical traditions. I am not sure what it is they think needs deciding; is it whether God is telling us the truth or that we must decide whether God will keep His promise to us? In any iteration of this hoary idea, there is a decided turning away from the much sounder tradition that God's grace is a gift to us, that we can do nothing to merit. This includes meriting by "deciding" in favor of God.

The second group is a distant relative of the Calvinists. They are the folks promulgating the prosperity gospel. As I outlined, the Calvinists held that you could establish that you had faith by doing good things. This morphed quickly into looking at prosperous people as faithful and less prosperous people as less faithful. In uniquely American fashion, the modern version of this is that if you have enough "faith," always evidenced by hefty tithing, then you will get good things in return. This is explicitly endorsing what my former pastor called the "slot machine Jesus model." Put your coin in, pull the lever, and get goodies in return. This too puts all the action on us and does so in a manifestly awful way. I will discuss in a bit the damage this can do to people's faith, but for now, it is enough to simply say ew.

So if you start down the wrong path (the forensic view of salvation), you see Christ as a means not an end, you will sooner rather than later arrive at a way of manipulating this means, then derive a list of things you need to do to obtain salvation. Add in a good portion of human awfulness, and you have a toxic stew of works righteousness, which is just self-righteousness. Self-righteousness, as in we can make ourselves righteous. It is clear by the historical evidence that there is a wide tranche of Protestants who, whether they admit it or not, subscribe to and preach a theology of works or, as Gerhard Forde put it, a "ladder theology."

So, why is any of this bad?

All right, we can see that much of the Protestant world, in addition to the formal dogma of the Catholic Church, adheres to some form of works righteousness. Is this the end of the world? Is this all that damaging?

I am not going to engage in a lengthy Scripturally based defense of the idea of salvation by faith alone in opposition to some sort of necessary works. Libraries are full of theologically sophisticated books on all sides of this issue. I will mention again that the idea that Christ is a means to the righteousness of God rather than God's righteousness Himself separates Christ from God in a way that is opposed to the creeds that those making this claim confess. It is also my position that Romans 3:28, "For we hold that a person is justified by faith apart from works prescribed by the law" means just that, using the interpretive framework set forth by Martin Luther and the other reformers.

That said, I am going to offer a street-level critique of the theology of works. I think this appropriate because most of the damage done by this outlook occurs in the application rather than the nuanced theological doctrines involved. First, I will offer a critique from the heart. I am not usually given to arguments from intuition, but they can be helpful. If a rule or teaching is so intuitively repugnant, then it behooves us to reconsider before we try to apply that rule or teaching to our lives. This is one of the ways I believe God speaks to us.

If we examine our hearts, we should understand very clearly that there is nothing we can or ever could offer God in the way of an external work that would make us worthy of His salvation. Salvation means an eternal relationship with God. In short, it means heaven, paradise, whatever superlative you wish to use. It means He gives us *everything*. What could we possibly do for God in exchange for that? If there is anyone notoriously difficult to shop for, it is God. I mean, what do you give the God who is, well, you know, God? None of us need to be biblical scholars to know deep in our hearts that there is nothing God needs from us and nothing we could offer Him anyway.

We know intuitively that we cannot manipulate God with works or gifts or bribes. We know instinctively that this is an unattainable goal, emotionally and physically. We simply do not have any hope that this is achievable. Goals that we have no hope of attaining are goals we quickly abandon. More than that, we are put off by those who tell us that we can attain this goal or who claim that they have attained it. *Self-righteous* is a pejorative term for a reason. We find this sort of person distasteful and often obnoxious. When we run into these sorts, we usually distance ourselves from them or at least ignore them. It is best not to ignore a piece of intuition that God has placed so deep in our hearts. One can see that an attitude that cuts so clearly against our heart's insight is an attitude that leads us away from an ongoing relationship with God.

This brings us to the other street-level argument against a theology of works: It produces disastrous results. This entire work, much of my life in fact is a testament to the damaging effects of works righteousness. Let's briefly review the path astray. The path astray often looks like this. First, you start to think that you have to follow some sort of law or rules to secure your salvation or climb a ladder as Forde put it. Then you begin to ponder what sort of standard you must meet to work your way into worthiness of God. Right away you realize that God's standard is perfection. This leads you likely to deem those preaching this theology of works, or ladder theology if you will, hypocrites since they are clearly not meeting this standard. For the record, these preachers are not hypocrites; they are simply human. It's the theology that sucks.

If that does not sour you on the gospel as being good news, you will likely begin to look at yourself as an unworthy hypocrite because you too are unable to meet this standard. Cognitive dissonance sets in, and you either meet the standard set, in this case perfection, which is impossible, or you chuck the whole standard and drift away from the faith altogether.

You may drift all the way to an explicit atheism as I did or to its functional equivalent in which you have no relationship with God at all. This is certainly not the path for everyone; however, it is the path for millions and millions of former Christians who have given up believing that there is any good news to be heard about Jesus.

That my case is not an anomaly is borne out by the significant amount of polling done on why people leave the Christian church and/or why people are not attracted to it.

At this point, it is not controversial to state that people are leaving the church in droves. This is true of all faith traditions but very pronounced among Christians. Recently published Pew Research shows that there has been a dramatic decrease in those who identify with a specific religion. In 2007, 78 percent of adults identified as Christian; in 2020, that number had dropped to 63 percent.

Meanwhile, those not identifying with any religion at all rose from 16 percent in 2007 to 29 percent in 2020. Notably, those identifying with other religions stayed basically flat going from 5 percent in 2007 to 6 percent in 2020. It is Christianity that people are fleeing.[19]

This decline has been concentrated within Protestantism. In 2007, 52 percent of US adults identified as Protestant, but by 2020, it was down to 40 percent. Catholicism, by contrast, only dropped from 24 percent in 2007 to 21 percent in 2020. Mormons and Orthodox Christians stayed relatively flat around 1–2 percent.[20]

It is easy to see that the decline has been steady and is concentrated among Protestants. After all the effects of a dogma of works righteousness combined with the sex abuse scandals, those who were going to leave the Catholic Church have likely already done so. This leaves the largest percentage decline among the Protestants. The only real debate is why so many are leaving. The consensus among Pew Research Center surveys is that most religiously unaffiliated people think Christians are intolerant. A 2016 Pew survey found that 46 percent of millennial respondents think Christians are generally less tolerant of others. Of those unaffiliated with any church, 36 percent became disenchanted with their faith. One top reason given was that "Too many Christians doing unchristian things"; that is, they are perceived as hypocrites. Among those who dislike organized religion, 20 percent of the unaffiliated, the top reason given was "I see organized religious groups as more divisive than uniting."[21]

A study published in 2019 by Lifeway Research, a Christian organization, revealed the main reasons young people left the church.[22]

- I moved to college and stopped attending church. 34%
- Church members seemed judgmental or hypocritical. 32%
- I didn't feel connected to people in my church. 29%
- I disagreed with the church's stance on social/political issues. 25%
- My work responsibilities prevented me from attending. 24%

The top reason, leaving for college is innocuous enough. However, the next three reasons reinforce the point I am making. Around 32 percent see members as judgmental and hypocritical. Around 29 percent are not connected to members of the church and 25 percent disagree with social or political stances taken by the church. All these reasons are connected to a theology of works righteousness. The hypocrisy charge has been discussed. Not connecting is a part of the general turnoff experienced by those whom they see as narrow-minded or bigoted. Disagreement with the church's stances on political and social issues is also a function of works righteousness as the stances themselves should not be a part of the core teaching of the church. If you hold that the good news is that Christ is risen and you simply believe, then political discussions come up but *outside* of the pulpit. On the other hand, if you think that there is a list of dos and don'ts that are core to your salvation, then you will tend to loudly insist on these and, in the process, turn off great numbers of people.

This survey was of people aged twenty-three to thirty, which is critical. If these people do not stay connected to God during these years, they likely never will. As generations go by, the more that are raised in families with just one parent of faith or none increases the odds of them not believing greatly. A Pew Research Center survey indicated that 51 percent of people raised by two religious "nones" are also religiously unaffiliated today.[23]

Less than half (45 percent) of millennials in another survey take their children to religious services regularly and only 39 percent enroll them in Sunday school. They clearly see no reason to be a part of what they consider to be an intolerant culture.[24]

The old church adage still applies today: So goes the youth, so goes the church.

Another interesting metric to show how far the rot has gone is a poll done by the Pew Research Center in 2020.[25] They asked people when the name of a religion was brought up, who came to mind. Catholics named the pope 47 percent of the time and Jesus came in second at 12 percent. Protestants named Billy Graham the most at 21 percent with Jesus tied for second at 5 percent with Martin

Luther. It is, I think, a measure of the earthly works focus of both Catholics and Protestants that Jesus garnered mention only 12 percent and 5 percent respectively.

It is not only the general population that is turned off by Christians; even some within the faith see the problem. One such insightful Christian is an evangelical pastor named Andy Stanley. He founded and still runs North Point Ministries, a nondenominational evangelical Christian church in the Atlanta area. His writings can be found on his website, yourmove.is. He rightly criticizes the notion that the Bible is the basis of Christianity. He rightly points out that Jesus is. He also corrects the notion that suffering disproves the existence of God, a particular problem for the prosperity gospel crowd. If life takes a big dump on you, as it inevitably will, then where does that leave your faith? You gave all the money and did the things you were told you should. Where are the nice things in return? This leads to predictably disastrous results.

Mr. Stanley also cites bad church experiences, not making people feel welcome and treating the church building as the church. At a basic level, he gets that it is about our belief, not the external things we do as an outgrowth of that belief.[26]

I know that many would respond to all of this with a big yawn. If people don't believe, goes the argument, it is sad, but we cannot water down the faith just to become more popular. My point is that we have *already* watered down the faith. We have done so by becoming disparate groups who claim that various external works are the key to our salvation. It doesn't matter if it is a set of left- or right-wing beliefs we must accomplish or adherence to the bureaucratic edicts emanating from Rome; it is all a deviation from the radical nature of the new thing that God did by giving us His Son, Jesus the Christ. It is not a case of adhering to a faith that others do not want to share, but rather, wandering so far down the wrong path that it is a wonder anyone at all wants to call themselves a Christian. It should surprise no one that so many are turning away from yet another group of hectoring rule minders who are little removed from the Pharisees Jesus so roundly criticized. Christians are losing the evangelical battle because so many have misunderstood what God has told us and are communicating a garbled message offering little real hope.

A new theology

Considering all that has been detailed in the data about why people are leaving the church, as well as my story as a microcosm for falling away and making my way back, it is time to formally call for nothing less than a re-reformation.

We need to junk erroneous theology, rid ourselves of the crude way in which this specious theology has been applied, and go back to what was distinct in the Reformation insight. That is, we need to go back to the pure joy of the good news. We need to recognize that all we need is to hear God's good and gracious word and *believe.* To state unequivocally that "For we hold that a person is justified by faith apart from works prescribed by the law." (Romans 3:28). Further, we should embrace Martin Luther's insight of the non-forensic view of salvation, that if we simply believe, then Christ, the righteousness of God Himself, dwells within us. There is really no reason the Christian community cannot coalesce around this simple yet profoundly powerful idea. Luther himself was not out to start a new church but to simply reform the existing church of Rome. It did not play out that way for a variety of theological and historical reasons, yet that goal remains a worthy one.

This means embracing a theology of grace, God's grace freely given. We can now boldly go forth, confident in our salvation apart from any external works. We can leave behind the cognitive dissonance of failing to meet God's standard of perfection. We can forget the feelings of hypocrisy toward those who preach this theology of works. We can never again see a hypocrite in the mirror because we too cannot meet that perfect standard. We never again have to step down the road I traveled toward unbelief and bitterness, and instead live in the light and warmth of a God that loves us and has totally forgiven us.

But what of works?

Okay, we have been saved by our faith. Now what? First, realize that if we are saved by faith alone, then a loss of faith is the only way we can lose our salvation. If no external work can make us worthy of God, then no external work can make us unworthy of God. Only by ceasing to believe can we break the relationship with God. Only by expelling Christ who dwells within us can we lose the righteousness of God.

Can we look at an external work and think maybe this person is not a believer? Yes, but we cannot be certain. Only God knows, and it is necessary to leave God's business to God. Only God can know the interior of an individual; there is no possible way we can.

The second thing to keep in mind is that there are such things as sins. Saved by grace through faith is not a license to do whatever we want and call it all good because we believe in Jesus as our risen Lord and Savior.

I am not going to go deep into a technical, arcane theological analysis of the nature and definition of sin. Remember, this is street-level theology. We all know in our hearts when we have done something wrong. We know in any given moment how we are to treat one another. We know not to steal, lie, spread rumors about people, or cheat on our spouses. The New Testament especially assumes that we know right from wrong. It is often Jesus's reaction; you know what you should do. Therefore, the New Testament is not a codex of rules and regulations; it is not another law book. It is a proclamation of Jesus as Lord and shows us Jesus's life as an exemplar of what it is to live a fully human life.

This points us to the still useful function of the law, a reminder when we have gone off track. When the law is at the right volume, it accomplishes this task. It then points us to the gospel, which makes us understand that we are forgiven and that we have Christ dwelling within us.

When the volume of the law gets turned up, it ceases to be the law and to serve a legitimate function. It becomes a tool of despair, harping on us that we are not good enough and will always remain unworthy of God. At this volume, it is a tool of a theology of works righteousness. We have seen where this leads, so we need to keep the volume down to a useful level.

When we are convicted by the law, at an appropriate volume, that we have done something wrong, then we should pick ourselves up, dust ourselves off, admit we screwed up, and remember that we believe and so are saved. We are defined by our sinfulness at a basic level (original sin), yet we are more defined by our saving faith in our risen Lord. This manifests itself in how we seek to treat one another. None of this is rocket science, nor is any of it unheard of to any of us. We seek to treat one another the way we would wish to be treated, to love one another the way God loves us, and to love God and love our neighbor. Who is our neighbor? Everyone. How often should we forgive one another? One more time than you think we ought to. When we fail to do this, we recognize it as sin, and therefore, need to recommit ourselves. None of these failures represents a break of faith that should ever cause us to doubt our salvation. This was the clear lesson I learned in my awful, sinful career experience I outlined in Chapter 9.

It is likely, though, that there will never be any formal reunification of the Christian world. Gone are the days of one church overseeing all the faithful. There has been too much history, too much rancor and emotion, and sadly too much distrust that remains. There is also too much earthy power and prestige at stake to think that this is an attainable goal.

That does not mean that we cannot achieve greater unity theologically. A re-reformation can focus on the idea of "faith alone." We can simplify the message down to its most crucial and essential truth, that we hear the Word and believe. We need not dive too deeply into the ancillary issues. We do not need to argue endlessly over technical theological issues such as the "real presence of Christ in the Eucharist," or the relative merits of consubstantiation versus transubstantiation, or whether the Holy Spirit proceeds from the Father or from the Father and the Son. This is all a diversion from the truth that is crucial: God sent His son; He lived, was crucified, and rose again. The good news is as simple as that: He is risen, He is risen indeed, hallelujah! Believe that and be confident in the indwelling of Christ within you (God's righteousness itself) and be confident of your salvation.

Enough about a rather negative response to our salvation. How can we and/or should we more positively respond to God's gift of saving grace? It is only natural after understanding what God is telling us and becoming secure in his salvific gift of grace upon grace that we want to know what to do now. The answer generally is that we naturally seek to express our gratitude for this gift. Again, we know the life God wants for us. We know how to go out positively and treat people well. It is not complicated yet not so easy for flawed humans to accomplish.

All of this will come naturally. The great Lutheran theologian and martyr Diedrich Bonhoeffer put it well when he said (I paraphrase) that if we believe, we will obey.[27] So much do I agree with this; it is why I named my website Believe and Obey. We will naturally seek to apply the gospel to our lives as best, if imperfectly, as we can.

The basic interpersonal way we treat others and respond to the world around us is what I would call the first stage of the applied gospel. The difficulty is in the second stage of applied gospel, the broader social questions regarding politics and policy, and make no mistake, Jesus's ministry was a social and political one. For instance, we can agree that we are to be stewards of God's creation, but it is how we best do this that bedevils us.

It is important to differentiate the merely important from the essential when thinking about our response to God's gift. The essential thing about Christianity is our belief in our risen Lord and Savior Jesus Christ. This *is* the gospel (which literally means good news). Our belief in this good news is the faith that saves us and sees Christ, the righteousness of God Himself dwelling in us. Our risen Lord obliterates all that stands between us and an eternal relationship with the Father. On this essential matter there can be no disagreement among Christians. If you don't believe this, you simply aren't a Christian. When we go into the sanctuary to worship and praise our risen Lord and Savior, there is not an inch of daylight separating us as Christians. I will discuss the ecumenical implications of this shortly.

This is true even though the form of worship may differ by various traditions. It is true if you are worshipping in a free form evangelical service or a more traditional liturgy, as found in the Catholic, Lutheran, or Anglican denominations. This shared belief is true even though there may be differences in denominational practice or dogma. Regardless of whether you believe there are two sacraments or seven; whether you believe the Eucharist embodies the real presence of Christ or is merely symbolic; whether your tradition practices infant or adult baptism, we are all unified by our belief that Christ died and is risen. It is *the* central belief that unifies all Christians everywhere. It is this which is essential and upon which we do not disagree.

This is in contrast with the "merely" important. Important issues arise when we attempt to translate how we are to live out our belief in our risen Lord. This is the realm of applied theology. This is the realm of politics and policy, social and cultural issues. Of course, these are important issues. They are the institutional means by which we treat one another, and God has everything to say about that.

It is in this realm, however, that we will always face differences and disagreements. People of various backgrounds and experiences will bring vastly different perspectives to these issues and will reach vastly different conclusions about what policy is most compatible with the gospel. The thing we must remember is that differing conclusions do not mean that the person holding those policy prescriptions are evil or unchristian. People of good faith and conscience can and will disagree.

The real threat to the Christian faith is not that people differ on matters of importance; the threat arises when people conflate the important with the essential. When people assume that important differences are essential, they risk shattering the faith. Indeed, much of the often sad, violent history of the church is driven by just this impulse. It is a path we must not tread any longer.

We must strive to continually separate the essential from the important. This does not mean we abandon those policy positions that we feel strongly about. We should be passionate in our beliefs and argue strenuously for those beliefs. We must, however, do so with love, patience, and civility. We must presuppose the good faith and intentions of those with whom we disagree. There are, I think, three key reasons this must be so.

First, to assume the good faith and intentions of our fellow Christians is itself Christlike. Jesus warns us against assuming ill motives (Mark 9:38–41). Jesus is willing to engage all sorts of people with all sorts of different perspectives and day-to-day beliefs. All He asks is an unyielding commitment to love God and your neighbor. To fail to heed this warning is to try to defeat people and not reach them, and Jesus never attempts this. If this is the path we go down, then we end the conversation before it ever begins, and this helps no one.

Secondly, to assume another's good faith and intentions is to open a dialogue in which you just might learn something. Life's greatest learning opportunities can be found by engaging with people of differing positions. Even if you don't change your position on an issue, just having to defend your current position and think about why you hold that view will educate you and make your thoughts clearer. If you end up changing your position, then you have learned as well. There is no downside to engaging in this kind of dialogue, but it can only be done with civility and the assumption of good intentions.

Thirdly, and perhaps most importantly, we should embrace a more generous attitude toward our political opponents because others are watching. There should be no doubt that the rest of the world watches how Christians conduct themselves in political and policy discussions, just as surely as your neighbor notices whether you leave the house on Sunday to go to church. If others see Christians as unable to have an adult conversation of these types of issues, why would they be attracted to find out more about the faith. On the other hand, if they see civility and generosity reign in these discussions, they just might take a step or two closer to the cross. A civil, adult conversation becomes a powerful tool for evangelization.

How awful would it be if someone seeking greater understanding of the faith was shut down because a current Christian did not think they had the "correct" position on some issue or other. Yet this happens all too often. Sadly, it even occurs among the clergy. It is beyond sad that we would risk turning someone away from Jesus because of a petty political difference rather than opening our arms to all who seek the Lord, as Jesus Himself did.

In the end, we should keep in mind the advice attributed to St. Augustine: "In fide, unitas; in dubiis, libertas; in omnibus, caritas" (In faith unity, in doubtful matters liberty, and in all things charity).

These disagreements are healthy and can be productive in the learning process. Productive, that is, if we show enough respect to talk *to* one another rather than *at* one another. These conversations are extremely important to the life of the faith community. But we must recognize that they will bring disagreement. This does not mean that it will bring disunity. If we can remember what is essential and treat each other the way we know in our hearts we are supposed to, then we can have a vibrant and useful conversation about these important issues.

It seems to me that if we are going to keep disagreement from turning into disunity, then pastors must refrain from having second-stage applied gospel discussions from the pulpit. I say from the pulpit because as citizens and participants in social life, it would be unreasonable to ask pastors not to participate in these second-stage applied gospel conversations altogether, as well as a great loss of perspective regarding these issues.

The purpose therefore of a sermon is to first proclaim what the good news is. This is the life, death, and resurrection of Jesus Christ. The way to do this is to discuss and help the faithful understand how Scripture reveals this. This then would lead also to a discussion of first-stage applied gospel (which belongs in the essential category) and a drawing of the broad outlines of how we are to act in the world in the name of our Lord and Savior as a response to His gift of grace. In other words, the broad outline of what God is asking of us using Jesus as *the* template for a fully human life, radical love, inclusion, peace, and forgiveness. This is quite enough of a task for any preacher.

The excessive focus by many in the pulpit on the second-stage applied gospel, for example, the Social Gospel folks, is that it quickly devolves into a theology of necessary works and leads us down the sad path that so many have trod. Part of a re-reformation is jettison-ing this type of thinking from the pulpit and relegating the import-ant second-stage applied gospel conversations to their appropriate forums. Or to paraphrase my former pastor, there is no Christian position [regarding politics]; there are many Christians with posi-tions but no Christian position.

All of this points to the main thing we must always keep in our minds, that we try to do good things *because* God has saved us, not *to* get Him to save us. It is a mindset. Are we doing things as a response to God's gift, or are we trying to curry favor with God? Like the state of someone's faith, it is not a matter we can see outwardly, but we can know whether someone is sticking around as a self-identified Christian or has simply given up. However, the consistent reframing of the issue of works in this manner can only improve the sorry state of today's church.

What this means for us individually is as varied as there are individuals. You may have a heart for teaching or for building houses for the homeless. Perhaps you have a calling to help feed those who are hungry. Maybe you are called to political activism. The choices are virtually endless. When you come to see good works as a response to God's gift, the specifics matter much less than you used to think.

Is unity possible?

Can we as followers of Jesus embrace a renewed focus of what is so new and radical in His message? Can we relegate the merely important to its proper sphere? Can we root out the insidious the-ology of works from the Christian movement, especially from a Protestantism still in deep denial? I have hope that it can be done. It is certainly my prayer that no one travel the road that I did and that any who has can find their way back to the cross. I do not think it will be a top-down effort, however. There are too many theologians and church leaders who have too much at stake in their existing theo-logical frameworks to let go easily, if at all. The real damage done by works righteousness occurred at the street level, and it is here that the battle can be successfully waged. In short, it must be a movement of the priesthood of all believers. The first thing we need to do is to insist upon a focus on the New Theology as I have defined it above.

The ancillary issues that have so divided Christianity can be set aside. Each faith tradition can embrace its own unique perspective on these ancillary issues. There is nothing inherently wrong with any of them. We can respect and even revel in the diversity that such traditions represent. What we can no longer compromise on is the aforementioned non-forensic understanding of our salvation. We must never again be tempted down the wrong fork in the road that sees Christ as a means and not an end. We have seen where this road leads, and it is not a healthy place for the followers of Jesus.

This re-reformation presents several immediate obstacles. Obviously, there is the case of the Roman Catholic Church and its formal dogma. There is also the Reformed tradition of John Calvin with its reliance on the forensic imputation model of salvation. There is also the issue of the more traditional/fundamentalist congregations and their decision theology. All of this may prove to be too much to ask of these folks. That does not mean we should not try.

First, let's consider the Reformed tradition within Protestantism. It is asking quite a bit of the heirs of John Calvin to walk away from the notion of God imputing His righteousness to us by means of Jesus Christ. However, no one should take the position that Calvin is infallible, or anyone else for that matter. Lutherans have rightly repudiated the awful and unsound things Luther wrote about the Jews. A whole host of various theological traditions have evolved over the centuries since the Reformation began. No one should dig in so deeply that they cannot embrace a differing perspective. In any event, it is not a wholesale repudiation of Calvin that is necessary, just a refocus of the notion of "through faith alone." Calvin certainly thought that we were saved by faith. All I am suggesting is a stronger formulation of what Calvin certainly believed. It is just a different angle on the problem, not a rejection of the core belief that is, out-wardly at least, at the core of Reformation theology. As for the rest of Reformed traditions, why should anyone be overly concerned about them? Again, revel in our diversity.

There is certainly no reason individuals raised in the Reformed tradition cannot come to understand hearing and believing and therefore seeing Christ as the end, not merely a means. They can take from their tradition that which comforts them, that which has been so much a part of their lives for so long. No one needs to give up that tradition to conceive of "through faith alone" in a different way. They certainly do not need to wait for theologians to sign off on a decree, which likely will never happen anyway. More importantly than seeing their faith differently, they can communicate it differently to those in their lives who may be curious. They will have truly good news to share and be more willing to share it.

There is equally no reason Lutherans should not embrace this renewed focus on the notion of faith alone. I mean, Lutherans above all should be willing to embrace the best of Martin Luther's theological insights. In fact, there is much greater hope that Lutheran theologians and pastors can embrace this as many already have. I have heard from the pulpit explicit sermons devoted to the notion of Christ dwelling in us because of our faith. I must admit, though, that it is beyond shameful that anyone associated with the Lutheran tradition should have wandered off down the forensic fork in the road. This should be the easiest movement in the Protestant tradition, yet even at that, it will not come that easily as old habits are hard to break.

The truth is that anyone, anywhere can embrace what is truly new and radical in Jesus's message. Anyone can understand what God is telling us and can respond accordingly. This is true not just of the Reformed or Lutheran traditions but any Protestant tradition, Methodist or Anglican, free-form evangelical or fundamentalist. At the street level, the priesthood of all believers can embrace this new perspective without giving up the totality of their traditions that they have known.

More importantly, anyone who has given up on the idea of hearing any good news about Jesus can embrace this perspective regardless of which tradition may appeal to them. You hear and understand, and you believe. The specific form of your response matters less than that you have the righteousness of God, Christ Himself, dwelling within you. At that point, you may return to a previous tradition,

seek out a new one, or be very intentional about finding a congregation that explicitly shares your new, enhanced understanding. What
is critical is that you simply believe and are therefore saved. A bottom-up clearer understanding can create a revolution in the church
and can serve as a crucial evangelical tool to bring people to the cross
for the first time and back to the cross for the last time. This is true
even if you do not respond by formally joining a congregation; as
much as I think that is so helpful.

The fractured nature of the Protestant tradition is certainly
an impediment at one level since it is difficult to get agreement on
issues. Then again, this diffuseness is an advantage because there is
no one centralizing authority to stop such a bottom-up movement.
In such an environment, we do not need to be on the altar to effect
change; we can do it from the pews.

Okay, what about the faith of my youth?

It is time to grapple with the behemoth of the Catholic tradition. For one thing, it is too large to ignore in any case. For another,
it has obviously played too large a role in my own experience. Time
to square up and clear my throat, so to speak.

First, I am not here to tell anyone not to be a Catholic. If you
are sincerely called to this tradition, then so be it. Who am I to tell
you different? Second, I recognize and have experienced firsthand
the power of cultural Catholicism. I understand the deep connection
that a lifetime of immersive Catholic experience brings. For many, to
not be Catholic would be like asking them to cut off their right arm.

Fortunately, the Catholic Church is not nearly so monolithic as
it would have people believe or as outsiders think it is. Any organization that has over a billion members and is over two thousand years
old is, whether it admits it or not, a big tent organization. There are
many wings to the Catholic Church and a whole lot of wiggle room.

There are many Catholic parishes in heavily African American
communities with the emphasis on emotion and especially emotive
music. This is the Baptist wing of the Catholic Church. There is a
movement in Catholicism known as the charismatic movement. My

pastor growing up made our parish a center of this movement in our area. Charismatics focus on raw emotion to the point of speaking in tongues. This is the Pentecostal wing of the Catholic Church. You like the old-school tradition of the low Latin Mass with the priest's back to you, that is RC classic. You can find a variety of differentiating traditions inside a huge and ancient structure such as Catholicism.

This leaves you a lot of wiggle room to live out a *sole fide* (faith alone) existence within the Catholic tradition. A wonderful place to start with this endeavor is a document titled *Joint Declaration on the Doctrine of Justification*,[28] which was published in 1999 by the Lutheran World Federation and the Catholic Church. It is available online on both Catholic and Lutheran websites (well worth the read, and only nine pages long). Notably, it was stewarded on the Catholic side by then Joseph Cardinal Ratzinger, later Pope Benedict XVI, a man not noted as a raging liberal.

I came across this document in 2004 and reread it while completing this work. I had no problem with it then, nor do I now. While the document acknowledges differences regarding a host of issues, not least is the nature of ecclesiastical and papal authority, there is stunning agreement on the core notions of justification. Early on in Section 2, the point is made:

> By appropriating insights of recent biblical studies and drawing on modern investigations of the history of theology and dogma, the post-Vatican II ecumenical dialogue has led to a notable convergence concerning justification, with the result that this Joint Declaration is able to formulate a consensus on basic truths concerning the doctrine of justification. In light of this consensus, the corresponding doctrinal condemnations of the sixteenth century do not apply to today's partner.[29]

I concur wholeheartedly. While I recognize the same theological differences that the authors of this statement did, I do not condemn the Catholic Church. Again, the nuances of technical theology are not the focus here. The street-level theology as it is applied is what I have been concerned with in this work. That is where the damage of works righteousness has occurred in both the Catholic and Protestant world.

To dive a bit further into this document, Section 15 states, "The foundation and presupposition of justification is the incarnation, death and resurrection of Christ. *Justification thus means that Christ himself is our righteousness*" [emphasis mine].[30] Further in that section: "Together we confess: By grace alone, in faith in Christ's saving work and not because of any merit on our part, we are accepted by God and receive the Holy Spirit, who renews our hearts while equipping and calling us to good works." Later in Section 37: "We confess together that good works—a Christian life lived in faith, hope and love—*follow justification and are its fruits.*" [again, emphasis mine][31] To all of this I can only say *amen*. There is no doubt that this was a document forged together by mutual love, respect, and the working of the Holy Spirit within all involved. If this had been published in 1520, there would have been no Reformation, nor much need of one.

It was so stunning that it produced predictable pushback amongst both conservative Lutherans and conservative Catholics. It is easier for decentralized Lutheran groups to ignore this if they choose but a bit harder for Catholics. One example of this is the conservative Catholic publication *First Things*, which on their website on March 12, 2010, published a response titled "A Betrayal of the Gospel: The Joint Declaration on the Doctrine of Justification."[32] Long story short, there was enough pushback that this document, while acceptable to the Catholic Church, is not a part of the magisterium of the church. This means that you do not have to believe it to be a Catholic in good standing.

But my point is you *can*. If what I have outlined here makes sense, if it speaks to you a new and radically different understanding of what God is telling us, yet you are now or wish to go back to the Catholic tradition, this document makes this possible. If you have greater clarity about simply believing, jettisoning all the baggage of trying to earn your way into God's good graces, you can grasp this document as your entryway to a Catholic tradition that may still be calling to you.

If enough enact this "revolution from the pews" in the Catholic tradition, then it is entirely possible that the documents produced by the Council of Trent may never be considered *de fide credenda* or a part of the deposit of faith and may continue to be considered *de fide tenenda*, a document contingent on historical events. It may even come to pass that the teachings that came out of the Council of Trent can be disposed of altogether. Remember my fear of the notion of limbo, where unbaptized babies go? It is no longer a part of Catholic dogma. Yes, the church does change, it has changed, and it can change.

Let me be even more bold; if you are called to be a Catholic, then, in the name of God, be one. If a clearer understanding of God's truth has renewed your spirit, yet for whatever reason you are called to the Roman Catholic tradition, then embrace it; do not fight it. You can indeed live a *sole fide* (faith alone) life as a Catholic and can be a part of a revolution from the pews. From within the Catholic Church bust out those windows and break down those doors and let some fresh air into this august institution. In the name of God, fight for her; she is still worth fighting for. I am under no illusions here; we need a strong and vibrant church of Rome to help us proclaim the love and saving grace of our Lord and Savior Jesus Christ. For all my issues with the street-level theological practices of the Catholic Church, I cannot deny the reality that I was named and claimed by Jesus the Christ in the Catholic tradition. I may be a Lutheran adult, but I was once a child of Rome, the importance of which I can neither forget nor take lightly. I have made my peace with Rome and will gladly work with any Catholic in the spirit of the *Joint Declaration on the Doctrine of Justification* for the furtherance of the gospel.

All God's children get weary when they roam

That line was penned by the late great singer-songwriter Joe South, in his work "Don't It Make You Want to Go Home?" The line captures, I think, the spirit of the moment. I perceive that the world is weary, and many are desirous of some good news. While the data suggest a growing group of "nones," as in not a part of a denomination or congregation, the data also suggest an overwhelming continuance of belief in God. People are still seeking something greater than themselves.

Many of God's children have indeed roamed far from home, and I cannot blame them. For too long they have heard a garbled, dispiriting message of judgmentalism and one that seems blatantly hypocritical. They have suffered the cognitive dissonance of thinking that they have to meet an impossibly perfect God standard while knowing in their hearts that they cannot and therefore assuming that they are not good enough for God. Any sane person would roam from that kind of misunderstanding, if only to get away from the drumbeat of thinking that you will never measure up. We instinctively distance ourselves from that kind of negativity because, well, who needs it?

With a clear understanding of what God is actually telling us, we can stop roaming and return home. Perhaps this means home to the faith tradition of your youth or home to a new faith tradition. It might mean coming home to a faith tradition for the first time ever. Whatever the specifics, it is my firm unshakable conviction that there are millions who, for the same or similar reasons to mine, walked and/or ran away from faith because of a repulsion at hearing a garbled message. This means there are millions who can benefit from hearing a clear message.

These millions can stop roaming, come home, cease being weary, and finally be a part of something greater than themselves—a something that is all-embracing, loving, and will provide the truth and joy of a life of unfathomably deep meaning. All it takes is the simplicity of hearing God's good and gracious word and believing, and accepting the forgiveness that God offers us all. From there I have no doubt that the Holy Spirit will take you to the response to God's gift that makes the most sense for you. The challenge is getting the clear, accurate message that God has been sending to humanity all along.

I am not naive. Spreading the clear, simple meaning of God's message will not go unchallenged. Preachers and entrenched faith traditions will conjure up a myriad of reasons there is some sort of "process" or to-do list, or "decisions" to make before becoming a part of the in-group. Our call is to ignore these naysayers who want to overly complicate and obfuscate God's simple, good word even if well intentioned.

Our call is to hear the word and believe. If you believe, then this will change you; I guarantee it. God will take any of us exactly as we are, but He will not keep us as we are. This change and our response to God's gift will not go unnoticed. People do notice what the faithful are doing. They see you pull out of the driveway to go to church; they pay attention to the way you treat others, and they pay attention to the way you respond to your belief.

This inevitably leads to conversations about what is going on with you. This presents all of us the opportunity to clearly and confidently proclaim that God loves all of us and wants a relationship with all of us, so much so that He sent His Son Jesus to live among us and to show us a path to an eternal relationship with the Father.

Your belief is all that is necessary for this eternal relationship. Gone is the awfulness of thinking or communicating to others that the Christian faith is all about meeting some unattainable standard. Gone is the charge of hypocrisy and the stench that charge leaves. All that is left is the proclamation to the world that you have heard the Word and believe and that anyone who hears and believes is welcomed home. This is the most powerful evangelical tool there is. God's simple truth, simply explained, all with open arms.

So what are the next steps?

Acting on this renewed and clarifying understanding of what God is telling us will take you home to a wondrous place. You will find yourself worshipping with those who also understand what God is saying or at least (as in the case of the Catholic Church, which I discussed above) allows you to understand it this way. I am convinced that this will grow the church once again. Will this bring unity? Probably not, but it does not have to.

Those with this clear understanding will find each other, and others will be drawn to this amazingly good news. We cannot be hesitant simply because some wish to hold to a discredited theology of works. We will, of course, love them and will always welcome them home if and when they hear God's message more clearly. On the other hand, if a unity is to be accomplished, it may come about because of a growing church. Nothing tends to unify so much as success. Regardless, all we can do is hear God's word, believe, and share as best we can. This can be the re-reformation that the world so desperately needs.

I will leave you with my most treasured passage in all of Scripture, which I think summarizes all that God had been telling us all along and all that I have tried to communicate in this effort, Mark 1:15, which states, "Behold the Kingdom of God draws near, repent and believe in the good news." Welcome home!

Praise be to God.

Notes

Chapter 1: Foundation and Framework

1   Jimmy Akin, "Faith and Works," Catholic Answers, accessed January 16, 2022, https://www.catholic.com/magazine/print-edition/faith-and-works-0.
2   J. Waterworth, trans. and ed., "The Council of Trent: The Canons and Decrees of the Sacred and Oecumenical Council of Trent," accessed January 16, 2022, http://www.documentacatholicaomnia.eu/03d/1545-1545,_Concilium_Tridentinum,_Canons_And_Decrees,_EN.pdf.
3   Gerhard Forde, *Where God Meets Man: Luther's Down-to-Earth Approach to the Gospel* (Minneapolis: Augsburg Publishing House, 1972).
4   Martin Luther, *The Small Catechism* (Minneapolis: Augsburg Publishing House, 1979).

Chapter 6: Lost in the Wilderness

1   George H. Smith, Atheism: The Case Against God (Amherst, NY: Prometheus Books, 1979).
2   Ibid., page xi.
3   On the topic of "sufficient causation," see Richard Taylor, *Metaphysics* (Englewood Cliffs, NJ: Prentice-Hall, Inc., 1983), chapter 10.

Chapter 9: Turns Out You Have to Keep Listening to God

1   Dietrich Bonhoeffer, *The Cost of Discipleship* (London: SCM Press, 2015).
2   Soren Kierkegaard, *Provocations: Spiritual Writings of Kierkegaard*, edited by Charles E. Moore (Walden, NY: Plough Publishing House, 2002).

Chapter 10: Toward a Re-reformation

1   *The Catechism of the Catholic Church* (New York: Doubleday, 1997), section 1471.

2   J. Waterworth, trans. and ed., "The Council of Trent: The Canons and Decrees of the Sacred and Oecumenical Council of Trent," chapter 10, accessed January 18, 2022, http://www.documentacatholicaomnia.eu/03d/1545-1545,_Concilium_Tridentinum,_Canons_And_Decrees,_EN.pdf.

3   *The Catechism of the Catholic Church* (New York: Doubleday, 1997), section 2010.

4   Phillip Cary, *Luther: Gospel, Law, and Reformation* (Chantilly, VA: The Teaching Company, 2004).

5   Forde, op. cit., 7–11.

6   Ibid., 11–12.

7   "U.S. Protestants Are Not Defined by Reformation-Era Controversies 500 Years Later," Pew Research Center, accessed January 19, 2022, https://www.pewforum.org/2017/08/31/u-s-protestants-are-not-defined-by-reformation-era-controversies-500-years-later/.

8   Neha Sahgal, "500 Years after the Reformation, 5 Facts about Protestants around the World," Pew Research Center, accessed January 19, 2022, https://www.pewresearch.org/fact-tank/2017/10/27/500-years-after-the-reformation-5-facts-about-protestants-around-the-world/.

9   Article IV of Justification, BookOfConcord.org, accessed January 18, 2022, https://bookofconcord.org/augsburg-confession/article-iv/.

10 Q & A 61–62, Heidelberg Catechism, Christian Reformed Church, accessed January 18, 2022, https://www.crcna.org/welcome/beliefs/confessions/heidelberg-catechism.

11 Amy Mantravadi, "Justification: The Reformed Protestant View," Reformation 21, Accessed January 18, 2022, https://www.reformation21.org/blog/justification-the-reformed-protestant-view.

12 "The Second Helvetic Confession," accessed January 18, 2022, https://www.ccel.org/creeds/helvetic.htm.

13 Josef Ehmer and Catharina Lis, eds., *The Idea of Work in Europe from Antiquity to Modern Times* (Burlington, VT: Ashgate Publishing Company, 2009).

14 Peter Marshall, *Heretics and Believers: A History of the English Reformation* (New Haven: Yale University Press, 2017), 239.

15 Sydney Ahlstrom, *Religious History of the American People* (New Haven: Yale University Press, 2004), 128.

16 Also providing excellent background is Francis Bremer, *Puritanism: A Very Short Introduction* (Oxford: Oxford University Press, 2009).

17 Walter Rauschenbusch (New York: The Macmillan Company, 1922).

18 Much useful background for this can be found in Murray Rothbard, *The Progressive Era* (Auburn, AL: The Mises Institute).

19 Gregory A. Smith, "About Three-in-Ten U.S. Adults Are Now Religiously Unaffiliated," Pew Research Center, accessed January 18, 2022, https://www.pewforum.org/2021/12/14/about-three-in-ten-u-s-adults-are-now-religiously-unaffiliated/.

20 Ibid.

21 Michael Lipka, "Why America's 'Nones' Left Religion Behind," Pew Research Center, Accessed January 19, 2022, https://www.pewresearch.org/fact-tank/2016/08/24/why-americas-nones-left-religion-behind/.

22 Aaron Earls, "Most Teenagers Drop Out of Church When They Become Young Adults," *Lifeway Research*, accessed January 19, 2022, https://lifewayresearch.com/2019/01/15/most-teenagers-drop-out-of-church-as-young-adults/.

23 "Links between Childhood Religious Upbringing and Current Religious Identity," Pew Research Center, accessed January 19, 2022, https://www.pewforum.org/2016/10/26/links-between-childhood-religious-upbringing-and-current-religious-identity/.

24 Daniel Cox and Amelia Thomson-DeVeaux, "Millennials Are Leaving Religion and Not Coming Back," accessed January 19, 2022, https://fivethirtyeight.com/features/millennials-are-leaving-religion-and-not-coming-back/.

25 Aleksandra Sandstrom and Becka A. Alper, "When Americans Think about a Specific Religion, Here Are Some of the First People Who Come to Mind," accessed January 19, 2022, https://www.pewresearch.org/fact-tank/2020/03/17/when-americans-think-about-a-specific-religion-here-are-some-of-the-first-people-who-come-to-mind/.

26 Andy Stanley, "Five Reasons People Leave the Church," accessed January 19, 2022, https://yourmove.is/five-reasons-people-leave-the-church/.

27 Bonhoeffer, op. cit.

28 *Pontifical Council for Promoting Christian Unity*, accessed January 19, 2022, http://www.christianunity.va/content/unitacristiani/en/dialoghi/sezione-occidentale/luterani/dialogo/documenti-di-dialogo/1999-dichiarazione-congiunta-sulla-dottrina-della-giustificazion.html.

29 Ibid.

30 Ibid.

31 Ibid.

32 Paul T. McCain, "A Betrayal of the Gospel: The Joint Declaration on the Doctrine of Justification," accessed January 19, 2022, https://www.firstthings.com/blogs/firstthoughts/2010/03/a-betrayal-of-the-gospel-the-joint-declaration-on-the-doctrine-of-justification.

About the Author

Since July of 2017, Tom Cleary has been writing weekly essays at his website believeandobey.net. In this role, he has covered many topics, such as scriptural commentary, various contemporary faith topics, and public policy issues from a radical Christian perspective. He has gained a dedicated following of those who wish to hear God's good and gracious word proclaimed in today's world. This writing effort is the product of over twenty years of scriptural study, both self-taught and under the tutelage of his pastors.

The author also brings real-world experience to his writing craft, as for over twenty-five years, he has had a series of sales and sales management roles in industries as diverse as coffee, financial services, and medical supplies. This perspective brings a street-level realism to his writing that infuses his work with a very accessible freshness.

Born and raised in Omaha, Nebraska, in the Catholic tradition, Tom went from faith to unbelief and back again after finally understanding what it is that God is saying to all of us. Married since 1994, Tom still resides in Omaha and is a father of two grown children and worships in the Lutheran tradition.